LEAD LIKE A WOMAN

WOMAN

Tenacious
Brought to you by Andrea Heuston

Featuring 16 Tenacious
Female Leaders

Lead Like a Woman: Tenacious

Published by Prominence Publishing

www.Prominencepublishing.com

ISBN: 978-1-990830-58-7

To Karina Autzen, Mandy Skey, and Effie Bar-Caspi. Thank you for always letting me be myself and loving me anyway.

Table of Contents

TABLE OF CONTENTS

FOREWORD

By Natasha Miller

TENACITY. TO DO WHAT MUST BE done to achieve something. Or as I put it, to punch through the glass ceiling, the boxes that are assumed and get to where *you* want to go, you must embody this. If you weren't "born with it" then develop, nurture and live it and get to be as tenacious as possible You'll need this. Tenacity is sometimes lopped into a similar negative category as the word "Relentless". I almost entitled my memoir "Relentless Tenacity" but went with the more simple *Relentless*. However, without tenacity, it would be difficult to have the spirit and energy to be tenacious.

Andrea Heuston as well as the other contributing writers of this book are tenacious with a capital "T". Some of their stories might resonate with you more than others. Some may look similar to your own. Others will be inspiring and give you insight on just how far we, as women, can actually go.

Writing a chapter for a book is yet another mark of tenacity. It's not for the faint of heart. There is pressure, bouts of imposter syndrome and a myriad of other mental roadblocks yet these women pushed through and made it happen. For you all to enjoy and learn from, so brava to them! And brava to you for picking this book up, supporting these authors and bearing witness to their stories.

"Lead Like a Woman: TENACIOUS" could be just what you need to bolster your own confidence and plump up your tenacious energy. Savor it and allow it to impact you in the most positive way possible. And begin to write your own chapter (or book) about how relentlessly tenacious you have been in your life.

Natasha Miller,
Founder/CEO Entire Productions Oakland, CA

INTRODUCTION

I'M SO EXCITED YOU'VE joined us for the third book in the *Lead Like a Woman* series. Our first two books in the series were so much fun to create and release. We received wonderful feedback and the stories have been shared all over the world, so I decided that it was time to write another one. For this new book, I went with the theme of **TENACIOUS**.

A few years ago, I was nominated for a business award. I was sent a form to fill out for a publication that would showcase my business. One of the questions on the form asked me to provide three words that describe me. I found the first two quite easily, but the third word was elusive. I could only think of the word *stubborn*. However, being stubborn is not generally looked at in a positive light. I called out across the office to my employee who had known me for over 10 years, "Carrie, what's a better way to say stubborn? I need a positive word to describe me!" Laughing, she instantly responded with the word ***tenacious***. And since I am quite tenacious, I was more than happy to adopt that adjective.

Tenacious *is* a positive term. If someone calls you tenacious, you're probably the kind of person who never gives up and never stops trying – someone who does whatever is required to accomplish a goal. Words like persistent, determined, and relentless come to mind. The stories in this book represent our collective tenacity.

Women in leadership positions often face challenges that men never will. These challenges require us to be tenacious. Many of these challenges center around our historical place in society – as caregivers. Family events and schedules often fall, by default, to us. For these reasons, it's especially important for female leaders to demonstrate both confidence and determination when it comes to business. These extra responsibilities are not justification for setting aside women under some pretense that they are delicate or distracted. Rather, they are compelling evidence of the tenacity we possess and our ability to act as leaders in all facets of life.

When we Lead Like Women, we demonstrate a belief in ourselves, in our worth, and in our own point of view. I encourage you to *Lead Like a Woman* in all areas of your life. Understand and know your worth, even when it feels like a stretch to get there. Do not rely on others' opinions of your life; your decisions and your journey are yours alone and they've created the person you are now, the person you'll become in the future.

Within the chapters of this book, you will get a chance to experience our determination, our relentlessness, our persistence. From overcoming obstacles such as hearing loss to fighting for family and business while a spouse lay dying, you'll understand how to pick yourself up and dust yourself off along the way. You'll get to read about reinvention, about business failure and success, and about having the relentless tenacity to go after what you want. These beautiful stories set the stage for success through learning.

There's so much good stuff in this book. *Lead Like a Woman: Tenacious* is full of real stories, real women, and real acts of unrelenting determination. The stories are heartbreaking and heartwarming. It takes you from childhood secrets to adult female power. We are warriors learning to harness our power of tenaciousness to create our futures and the futures of those around us.

Enjoy every chapter, every story of bravery, and yes, stubbornness. This book is the third in the series of *Lead Like a Woman* books, with more to come. I'm excited to share these stories with you about women who have overcome, forged ahead through fire, and dared to be too much.

Be brave, take risks, defy convention!

Leading Like a Woman Always,
Andrea Heuston

CHAPTER 1

The Tenacity of Motherhood

She wore her scars as her best attire,

a stunning dress made of hellfire.

– Daniel Saint

By Andrea Heuston

ERIC AND I MARRIED IN 1994, and we started talking about having children about three years in. Some of our friends were down that path already, and we thought we'd explore it, too. I was 26, Eric was 25, and kids just seemed like the natural next step for us.

I'm stereotyping now, but I believe most of us think getting pregnant is just going to be easy. I remember thinking, "Okay, well, here we go. Next month, we'll be pregnant."

I came by that belief naturally, being raised in a religious household where sex before marriage was a no-no, and reinforced by the knowledge that my dad had had a surprise baby and forced first marriage when he was a young man in college.

My belief was that the minute Eric and I tried to have kids, we would get pregnant; it would be a no-brainer, and it would be done. This getting pregnant thing must be a breeze, right? It just happens.

Yeah. But it didn't. It absolutely didn't happen that way.

We tried without success for about a year before we decided to begin exploring what was going on. We started doing things like checking my basal body temperature, so we'd know when I was ovulating and fertile. I'd always had issues with my periods. They were brutal and painful and would put me in bed some days, but at the time, we didn't really think anything of it.

I made an appointment with my OB-GYN, who put me on Clomid, which modulates estrogen and is often the first step in getting pregnant. The protocol at the time was Clomid for six months, and if nothing happened, we'd move to the next step.

Hot flashes happened, but I did not get pregnant.

We moved on to seeing a fertility specialist. We originally started with my OB-GYN, but after a year and a half of trying, I had to drag myself there for appointments. Seeing pregnant bellies and newborn babies in the waiting room was much too frustrating and sad. It made it hard for me to continue.

In 18 months, I'd gone from excited and whole to feeling depressed and defective. The one thing that I can say about infertility in general is that it was like a death every month when I didn't get pregnant. Each month, I was primed for life, and each month, I grieved the life that didn't take hold and grow.

It took a mental and emotional toll on me. Particularly because my early life had taught me that having children was the natural course for a woman. It's what I was meant to do. I was supposed to bear children. I was not living up to expectations. In essence, at my emotional core, I felt like I'd screwed up.

We chose to try a fertility clinic in downtown Seattle and started the next steps, one of which was clearing my fallopian tubes. They put me on an operating table and shot water and dye through my tubes. It was one of the most painful things I've ever experienced. Eric said I practically levitated off the table.

What we learned in the process—and was really confirming for me—is that it was me that was broken, not Eric. He was fertile. I just could not get pregnant.

One of the doctors told me that I would have been fertile if I'd gotten pregnant at 12 and that my eggs were old by the time I was 22. We tried working with my old eggs for over a year through a series of Intrauterine Insemination (IUI) procedures. I took a bevy of fertility drugs that caused a 50-pound weight gain, and I still couldn't get pregnant.

This was back before social media was a thing, and I'd found a website and chat from the InterNational Council on Infertility Information Dissemination (INCIID). It was the one place I could share my story with women who understood it, and they could share theirs. It was fascinating and fabulous and scary and sad, all at the same time.

We had decided at that time to look for a specialist in Invitro Fertilization (IVF). I asked for referrals on INCIID and found one of the foremost fertility doctors in the country. Dr. Kevin

Sullivan came highly recommended, and we decided IVF with him was our next step.

By this time, I was nearing 30, feeling like a defective old pin cushion, and really, like this was never going to happen.

You know, married couples either get closer together over infertility or are split wide apart. Although it didn't feel like it at times, it truly brought Eric and me together.

During this part of the journey, I had near constant blood draws and injections. Even my veins were tired of it. They started rolling away. One day, I had blood taken from my forehead and another day, from my foot. Those were the only veins they could find. Eric gave me shots in my butt and shots in my stomach area for months on end just so that we could create eggs to have a baby. It was a difficult time, but we did it because we both really wanted kids. We wanted to be parents.

We knew we could afford exactly one round of IVF. Twenty years ago, IVF cost around $20K and was not covered by insurance. So, we sold things. We saved pennies. We did everything we possibly could to get the money together.

IVF affected my body strangely. My ovaries blew up with eggs, which was an unusual response for someone with old eggs. They'd harvested eggs from me before, but not to the same degree.

On the day of insemination, I had seven fertilized eggs. None of them had made it to the blastocyst stage, but the doctors still thought they might. So, they put all seven of those almost-embryos back into my body and waited.

And. Not. A. Single. One. Took.

I was so devastated I don't think I talked to anyone for weeks. We'd spent $20,000 and years of our lives. The physical, mental, and emotional toll was brutal. And we got nothing from it. That's how we felt.

The doctors said, "Well, you know, you can try again in a year. Things are improving all the time." Another round was not in our financial or emotional budgets.

It was October of 2000 when we decided to give it up. We were done.

I went to a deep and dark place for a long time. The voice in my head, which was speaking directly from my upbringing, said a woman was supposed to have a child and stay at home to parent that child.

I couldn't do the one thing that I was put on earth to do—give birth to a baby. And I couldn't do anything about it. God knows we'd tried everything. Of course, it wasn't my fault. It wasn't anybody's fault. But I'd created a victim story around it and blamed myself anyway. I believed it, and I lived in it.

I lost some of my sense of self during that time. I'm not a shy person, but I became more introverted. I became more dependent on other people, and I worried more about what other people thought of me.

For five years, I told people I was defective. I actually said those words. "I can't have a baby. I'm defective." "Um, sorry, husband. You shouldn't be with me if you want a family." I wore my pain and brokenness on my sleeve like a blinking badge of honor. See, I screwed up. It's all my fault. I became my own limiting belief. I beat myself up instead of loving myself.

I know now that I unintentionally chose—and it was a choice, albeit unconscious—to think of myself as broken. As defective. As a victim of my circumstances. Was it an understandable reaction?

Yes. I was exhausted. Tired to my pin-cushioned bones. Beat down.

My friends have often heard me say that I wouldn't wish infertility on my worst enemy. Well, adoption is no picnic, either.

It wasn't long before we decided to move in that direction. With several adopted family members, including my brother Ryan and my grandmother, it was a natural progression for me. Of course, people in our family and friend circles had their own opinions about it, but I'll just share Eric's because it's my favorite. When someone asked him if he really wanted to open his family to a child that's not his blood, he said, "My wife is my family, and she's not my blood, either." So there.

We went to an adoption fair at a local hospital and were matched right away with an attorney we really liked. We thought we'd go for a private adoption and avoid going through an agency. There's a cost and process differential that felt right to us at the time. I'm sure you can imagine how excited we were when we matched with a birth mom right away. But, when she was about three weeks away from giving birth, she backed out.

We were torn apart all over again.

Despite this, we moved forward. On the advice of some friends we met through an adoption support group, we joined an agency in Spokane, which is about five hours away from where we live, just outside of Seattle.

By January, we were matched again, but before I share more about that, I have to say that the whole process of getting to that point rubbed me the wrong way and pissed me off. We basically had to create a portfolio of our lives, a marketing tool to sell ourselves as potential parents.

I mean, you know, the world is full of people who conceive and give birth every day. There are no parenting requirements for them. It's fair, too, to say that we all know people who probably shouldn't be parents for various reasons, and they have kids without restriction. And then there are people like us who cannot have babies and must also learn to jump through all the hoops required to get approval to adopt a baby. I'm not saying it shouldn't be that way; I'm just saying it infuriated me.

We hired an adoption consultant so we'd know all the right answers. We didn't want to say the wrong thing (such as we believe in spanking...we don't, btw) and have some stranger decide we couldn't have a baby. We did a home study, provided credit reports and financials for the last five years, gave references, and on and on. It was absolute insanity.

But by January, we were matched with two birth moms, and the agency didn't give us a choice. They said, this birth mother came in first, so this is who you're matched with. Come over and meet her.

I'm going to refer to our birth mother as Jen (not her real name) for the sake of privacy. Jen was three months pregnant at the time we met her. Her grandmother was very instrumental in creating a safe space for this adoption. Jen's mother had been adopted and was very anti-adoption and not supportive of it. Her grandmother, however, was utterly behind it.

Now, Jen had a backstory. I've learned over the years to take everything she says with a nod and a smile and an awareness of

"Who knows what's true?" She told us that she had been kicked out of the house by her mom when she was ten and had been homeless ever since. She was 19.

We worked hard on a relationship with her. I went over to Spokane (a five-hour drive) for doctor's appointments. Jen had done a full background study that's designed to ensure that everyone is informed and aware of all situations and that the adoption will go through and all will be well. As we had already learned, it's heartbreaking for everyone involved when something happens to stop it at the last minute.

When Jen was eight months along, we got a call from the state. They told us that, somehow, some arrest records had been overlooked and that Jen had been drunk while she was pregnant, and they said, "We know she uses drugs, but we don't know which ones." As soon as I got off the phone, the agency called me and said you may want to reconsider this adoption.

Eric and I had already named the baby. I'd been to every doctor's appointment, and because it was an adoption and Jen was high-risk, we'd seen our son multiple times through ultrasound. We already felt that we were his parents. Eric and I spent about 48 hours talking, discussing, and thinking. We called the agency back and said we wanted to move forward.

And then Aidan was born.

I remember that morning so vividly. It was early—6 a.m.—on June 28 (Aidan was due on July 10). I was feeling sick with a sore throat and was planning to work from home.

Eric had already left the house for work, and five minutes later, the phone rang. It was Jen. She said, "I'm in labor. I'm leaving for the hospital. How soon can you get here?"

I called Eric, who was at the coffee stand across town, and he said, "I'm turning around. I'll call my boss." He got home, we threw on clothes, grabbed a bag, and made the five-hour drive to Spokane in three and a half hours. We averaged a hundred miles an hour. Thank God we didn't get stopped.

We arrived at 12:02 p.m., and Aidan was born at 12:14 p.m. I held one of Jen's legs while she gave birth to Aidan. Eric cut the cord, and they handed the newborn to me. And we had a baby.

I have the first photo of Aidan, Jen, and me. We're both looking at the camera, and tears are just streaming down our faces.

Jen didn't want Aidan in her room, and they wouldn't let us in the nursery. We had to get a lawyer and petition to be allowed in. Six months later, the adoption was finalized in court. According to Washington state law, during the first six months, the birth mother can change her mind and come take the child away. We were completely and totally bonded to Aidan. Thank God Jen didn't make that choice.

For a few years, I sent yellow roses to Jen on Aidan's birthday. When he was one, she got yellow roses. When he was two, she got yellow roses.

By this time, Aidan was a miracle. He walked one day and ran the next, right before his first birthday. He hardly ever crawled. He was communicating with us in sign language by six months old. He knew milk, more, please, thank you, and Mom at six months. By nine months old, he had words. Aidan was a crazy smart child.

When Aidan turned three, I couldn't find Jen. We had lost her, which meant she was likely homeless again. So, I called her grandmother, Mary, and said, "Mary, I am trying to find Jen. I'd like to send her flowers, as I always do." She said, "Just a minute, Andrea." I thought she was going to get Jen's new address for me, but Jen picked up the phone.

I wasn't prepared for that at all or for the next words out of her mouth. "Hi, Andrea. Do you want another baby?" I wondered if she was talking about her daughter, that she'd given birth to six months after Aidan was born.

I said, "Um, well, tell me what's going on?" And Jen said, "I'm pregnant. It's a boy, and the baby is due on August 27." This was in early June of 2004.

Well, August 27th was our 10th wedding anniversary, and without pausing to hang up the phone and call Eric, I said, "Yes, of course we'd love to have another baby."

I got off the phone with her, called Eric, and said, "We're going to have a baby boy." He replied, "Andrea, I did not think that was possible. What are you talking about?"

We got in the car that weekend with our three-year-old and drove to Spokane to meet Jen and the birth father. Then, for the next two and a half months, I proceeded to attend all the doctor's appointments in Spokane. Every time I went, my dear friend Mandy flew with me. Her husband worked for Alaska Airlines at the time. She had free flights, and we both flew for free. I was blessed to have her support.

Owen was due on August 27th but came early on August 21st. It was an entirely different experience. In the three years since Aidan had been born, the hospital had become more adoption-friendly, and we had immediate access to him.

We were in the room for Owen's birth, and Eric again cut the cord, but a nurse swept Owen out of the room immediately. He'd been born too cold on the Apgar scale, and he was blue. (Apgar is a scoring system designed to quickly summarize the health of newborn children.)

A few minutes later, the nurse came back with the bundled-up baby in her arms and said, "Mom, take off your shirt." I looked at Jen, and the nurse said, "No, Andrea. You're the Mom. Take off your shirt."

I removed my shirt and bra, and the nurse nestled Owen in on me and wrapped both of us up in hot blankets. So there, the three of us sat with this new baby, and again, tears streaming down our faces. And I'm the Mom. It was such a powerful thing.

And Eric and I have two beautiful sons.

When we adopted Owen, we almost didn't get him. The birth father changed his mind the night Owen was born and said, "I'm not giving the baby up. I'll take care of him." He had neither a job nor a place to live, and a social worker got him to understand that if the baby didn't come to us, he would go into foster care. So, he did relinquish custody, but it was touch and go for six months. He and Jen are no longer together.

The minute I first held Aidan in my arms, I was like, "Oh my God, I'm his mom." In that moment, it wasn't about me. It was about him. It was absolutely not about me and my experience getting there. It didn't matter how I got there. What mattered was I was there, and I was a mom.

The same thing happened with Owen. He became mine when we sat skin-to-skin, wrapped in hot blankets.

I no longer feel like we got nothing. We got everything.

I am the mom of these two amazing young men whom I love with all my heart, beyond whatever capacity I once thought was possible. It doesn't matter if my kids came through me or to me. They're my heart. Our boys are our boys.

Our family is complete. Eric and I have two beautiful, wonderful, incredible sons.

About the Author

Andrea Heuston, the dynamic CEO of Artitudes and the force behind the Lead Like a Woman Movement, brings her vibrant personality, creative expertise, and speaker coaching skills to every endeavor. With a passion for communication and a knack for captivating audiences, she transforms ordinary presentations into extraordinary experiences. As a successful entrepreneur, Andrea understands the unique challenges faced by female business leaders.

With over 30 years of experience in the tech industry, Andrea started "The Lead Like a Woman Show" podcast in 2020. The show charts internationally on a weekly basis and has over 40,000 followers on social media. The Lead Like a Woman

Show focuses on empowering female leaders to empower others through topical discussions and interviews.

Andrea is passionate about helping to close the gender gap for women in business and she has a goal to help 1 million women own their stage by April of 2031.

Connect with Andrea:

http://AndreaHeuston.com

http://Leadlikeawoman.biz

LinkedIn: AndreaHeuston

CHAPTER 2

3 Magic Words: A Journey Through Life's Trials

By Fran Biderman-Gross

LIFE HAS A WAY OF THROWING curveballs when you least expect them, and sometimes, these curveballs can redefine our entire existence. This is a story about one such defining period in my life—a time that pushed me to the brink but also revealed strengths I never knew I had. At the heart of my journey are three simple words my father said to me in a moment of sheer exhaustion and despair. These simple yet powerful words became my anchor and continue to guide me and help me navigate life's toughest challenges.

At the age of 31, my life was comfortably full. I married David, my partner in both life and business, and we navigated daily joys and challenges together. We were raising two wonderful children, Avinoam and D'vora, whose laughter and energy filled our home with lively, loving chaos. Professionally, David and I ran our own print and promotional business. His ability to connect with clients paired well with my knack for managing the details, making us a solid team. Together, we built a company that not only supported our family but also reflected our joint efforts and commitment.

One day, out of the blue, David began to complain of back pain. This was unusual since he had never suffered from back issues before. We initially joked about how, even in our early 30s, it seemed we weren't escaping the aches and pains of getting older. But as the pain persisted and even intensified, our concern grew. David saw several doctors, but none could pinpoint any specific issue. Determined to get to the bottom of this, we continued seeking answers, hoping to alleviate his discomfort and return to our regular lives.

One doctor, puzzled by David's unrelenting discomfort, suggested we check deeper. A full body scan was needed - a test we hoped would finally give us some answers. The results led to an appointment I'll never forget—I remember every detail about that day: the office we were in, what I was wearing, and even the brisk chill that seemed to pierce through the window. The doctor's voice was somber as he broke the difficult news: it was a cancerous tumor pressing on David's sciatic nerve. David was a healthy man with cancer. The doctor paralyzed us with disbelief as he recommended that his leg be amputated.

This meeting marked the end of our old life and the beginning of a new, daunting chapter. What we had brushed off as possibly minor back pain was actually a life-threatening cancer. We were suddenly thrust into a battle for David's life, a stark contrast to the everyday challenges of managing work schedules and juggling kids' activities.

This harsh new reality instantly overshadowed our everyday worries, one where hospital visits and treatment plans became our new norm.

Our situation was severe. David's cancer diagnosis was not just alarming; he had an aggressive, vicious type of cancer. Had we detected it earlier before it spread, perhaps the outlook might have been different. The "what-ifs" haunt me until this day — what if we had found it sooner? The reality was harsh; it had

3 MAGIC WORDS: A JOURNEY THROUGH LIFE'S TRIALS

already spread, leaving us with a grim prognosis. This truth fueled my relentless search for any possible trials worldwide that offered a glimmer of hope.

Suddenly thrust into the role of David's primary caregiver, I was swimming in uncharted waters. The task demanded that I dive into the depths of medical research, relentlessly pursuing the most promising new treatments and clinical trials across the globe – anything to stop the monster in its tracks. I spent so many nights scouring the internet when my body needed sleep, but it's like running out of air while swimming deep in a pool ocean – you furiously kick to the surface regardless of how tired your legs are.

I had to search for anything that could offer hope.

So much of the year after David's diagnosis is a blur in my memory. I was constantly balancing the demands of David's care with the emotional and physical needs of our children, who were just 10 and 6 at the time. There was the daily routine of homework and school events, juxtaposed with David's lengthy chemo treatments and inpatient hospital stays. Additionally, the pressure to keep our business afloat was immense. Since we worked together and relied solely on this income, failing to maintain the business meant risking everything we had built.

Perhaps the most challenging aspect was providing unwavering support for David. Despite how much my own world was turned upside down, I had to remember that this ordeal was unfolding directly to him. Maintaining a brave face required immense emotional strength, especially when the extensive research I conducted daily revealed grim realities about his condition that he wasn't aware of. Each day, I had to compose myself and radiate positivity, a task that was both exhausting and essential. I had to keep hope alive for both David and our children.

I'm not sure how I would have survived that tumultuous period without the support I received from my family, friends, and community.

The gestures of kindness came in various forms and were deeply appreciated. For instance, parents of my children's classmates would often step in to take them to activities, providing a much-needed (mental) relief when I had to be at the hospital with David as they relieved me from worrying about the children and the guilt of not being able to be in two places at once. Similarly, the unexpected arrival of meals or groceries at our doorstep was an appreciated gesture and a profound reminder of the thoughtfulness and care of those around us.

But honestly, the cornerstone of my support system was my father. It might sound cliché, but he was my rock throughout this entire ordeal. He was always there for me, regardless of the time of day. He spent countless hours with me in hospital waiting rooms, offering his presence as a source of comfort and stability. To say he was there for me would indeed be the understatement of the year. He was more than just supportive; he was the crutch I leaned on when I felt too weak to stand on my own. His unwavering presence and encouragement helped carry me through the darkest days, reminding me that no matter how challenging the journey, I was not facing it alone.

And then, the most unexpected and shocking thing happened.

One day, I stopped by the office to check on things. The mail had just arrived, so it was the first thing I picked up. I shuffled through the usual assortment of bills and notices – nothing unusual—until I came across the bank statement. Figuring I'd give it a quick glance before returning to a mountain of other tasks, I started sorting through the enclosed cashed checks, checking them off against the statement.

As I was going through them, something caught my eye. One of the checks didn't seem right. It was made out for $3,000, a significant sum, and was written to our office administrator. That was odd. Why would she write a check to herself? Trusting her as part of our extended family was meant to ensure that our business operations could run smoothly in our absence, relying on what we believed was a dependable and trustworthy arrangement.

There was no reason for her to write a check to herself. My heart started spinning, and my mind started racing as I flipped through more checks. Then I found another, and then another, each penned in her unmistakable handwriting, made out and my signature forged. Each check was written to her for similar amounts. I felt a chill run down my spine.

What was going on? Why were these checks written to her? Panic began to set in as I realized this could only be one thing. I looked up and smiled at her, then walked casually into David's office and closed the door. I needed to think and needed to get out of her line of sight.

Once I closed the door behind me, I laid everything out on David's desk and began to sort through it all. The numbers just weren't adding up. There were obvious mistakes in payments made that needed to line up directly with our records. My stomach twisted as I realized what was happening—she was stealing from us. Feeling shaky, I picked up the phone and called my dad. "Dad," I said, my voice trembling, "I think my administrator is stealing from us." He was calm, which was such a contrast to how frazzled I felt. He told me to carefully collect all the evidence and reassured me that we'd figure this out together. Hearing his steady voice was a bit of a relief, but the weight of what I'd just found out was crushing. How long had this been going on? How much had she taken? How can someone, who we consider to be like family, exploit our fight for David's life? How was I going to find someone I trusted to run our business when we were hardly ever there? This experience felt like the final straw.

I sank deep into my chair, put my head in my hands, and whispered to my dad, "I can't do this anymore." "Yes, you can," he replied. "Just ten percent more. You can give it just ten percent more; I know you can." After taking a few deep breaths, I hung up and went back into the main office. I spent a few more minutes on my desk, collecting anything I thought I might need, forced a smile, and thanked her for 'holding down the fort.'

I asked if she needed anything, and I gathered my things to leave, keeping up appearances despite the turmoil inside.

The next steps were a blur. I contacted the bank to put a stop on any further questionable transactions and arranged for a thorough audit of our books. As the investigation unfolded, it became clear that she had been embezzling funds for several months and only after David's diagnosis arrived. She had exploited our trust and the chaos of David's illness, perhaps believing that we were too distracted to notice.

The betrayal cut deep. Here I was, already fighting on every front to keep my family and our business afloat, and now this. It felt like too much to bear. This wasn't just about money; it was about the betrayal of someone I had considered part of our extended family. It was a stark lesson in vigilance and trust, one that I would not soon forget.

But out of everything, there's that one moment that really sticks with me—the time I thought I was completely done for, and my dad gently reminded me, "You can give it just ten percent more." That little nudge was all it took. Those words, "just ten percent more," have stuck with me ever since. Whenever I've felt like I had nothing left to give, when it seemed like the tank was empty, those words would pop back into my head. They've pushed me to find that little extra something to keep going and to do what needs to be done, no matter how exhausted or depleted I felt.

It wasn't just that these were encouraging words; it was more like my dad was pointing out the strength he knew I had inside me, reminding me to tap into it. "Just ten percent more" became my mantra that has replayed in my head throughout my life. It helped light the way when things got really tough. It pushed me to dig a little deeper, to pull out that bit of extra strength I needed when everything seemed just too much. This mindset didn't just help me get through the day-to-day challenges of looking after David and keeping our business going during such a hard time; it totally changed how I see tenacity. For me, tenacity leads to resilience. I came to understand that being tenacious gives me the strength to be resilient. It isn't about avoiding pain or staying untouched by life's hard knocks. It's about facing up to those challenges, getting through them, and coming out the other side stronger, more flexible, and ready to take on whatever comes next. You must dig deep to know what you need to get through it all.

While the situation unfolded, we were grappling with David's decline. The total stolen reached over $30,000, a substantial sum significantly impacting our business during an already vulnerable time. We were forced to involve the police, leading to an investigation and eventually her arrest. Dealing with the police investigation and an arrest was a surreal experience. Despite the betrayal, a part of us felt terrible about the consequences she faced. It was a difficult position to be in, knowing that our actions to protect our livelihood were simultaneously upending someone else's life, someone we had once trusted and cared about. This mixture of necessary action and regret was a stark reminder of the complexities of handling betrayal.

This experience taught us a crucial lesson about the delicate balance of trust and oversight in business. You must inspect to expect. We learned that no matter how close someone is or how much they are trusted, it is essential to maintain proper checks and balances. This wasn't just about financial security; it was about protecting the integrity and future of our family and business. But the worst part of this timeframe is that David was losing his battle with cancer, and this situation added to my already significant stress.

Then, in the summer of 2001, David peacefully passed away at home. He was 33.

After David died, I was bereft. That is such an understatement for my age and stage of life.

You get so lost in the fight that you really don't let your mind drift to what comes "after." I wanted to be alone with my grief and just hide in bed, but my kids were 12.5 and 7, and that wasn't an option. I needed to redefine what our life would look like now without him.

The days following were a blur of trying to keep things normal for the kids while inside, everything felt broken. That's when the mantra of "just ten percent more" started popping into my head. It wasn't just about doing a little more work or spending an extra hour awake; it was about pushing through when all I wanted was to stop. It reminded me to take small steps, whether managing our morning routine or simply cooking dinner when I only wanted to collapse. It helped me to see what was right in front of me versus what was ahead in the distance.

This mantra helped us adjust to life after David. It was about finding that extra bit of energy to attend the school play, help with homework, or listen to my children talk about their day. It pushed me to find moments of happiness and normalcy for them, even when grief made it tough even to smile. It gave me the courage to travel with them alone. Every time I thought I couldn't do it and couldn't handle being both mom and dad, those words "just ten percent more" nudged me forward. They became a quiet force, guiding me to build a new path for us, filled with hope and the possibility of happiness, even when I thought it was out of reach.

A particularly poignant moment in our journey was the Bar Mitzvah of our son. This event, deeply embedded in Jewish tradition, marks a boy's transition into adulthood. Planning and executing such an event just six months after our profound loss was both a challenge and a form of healing. It required organizing a significant celebration and a great deal of emotional strength. The occasion was bittersweet, highlighting David's absence, yet it also affirmed life, showcasing the resilience of the human spirit and celebrating the continuation of our family's story.

I had to begin the planning while David was still alive. By then, he was a mere shadow of the vibrant person he once was, lying unconscious in his hospital bed due to the intensive chemotherapy. The contrast between planning this celebration of growth and new beginnings while dealing with our deep personal loss highlighted the complexity of our emotions. However, through this significant milestone, we found a way to honor David's memory, allowing ourselves to experience the joy of the occasion amidst our grief.

I share my story in the hopes that it reaches others who are also walking through their own tough paths. Whether it's taking care of someone you love, feeling the deep pain of loss, or facing the tough job of putting your life back together after everything's fallen apart, the key is realizing that the tenacity inside of you is never too far out of reach. It's about digging deep to find that "ten percent more" within ourselves and using it to take one step forward and then another, moving forward day by day. By doing this, we honor those we've lost, celebrate the strength we've found, and are open to new beginnings and the never-ending strength of the human spirit. When it feels like there's nothing left, there's always a way to give just "ten percent more."

About the Author

Fran Biderman-Gross is an expert in building strong brands, creating effective marketing strategies, and guiding clients through a valuable journey of culture discovery. Since its inception, Fran has used her 3 Keys Technique to contribute to the enduring success of hundreds of companies.

Fran is passionate about helping people stand out so that their full potential can shine. She is also the co-author of the well-received book "How to Lead a Values-Based Professional Services Firm: 3 Keys to Unlock Purpose and Profit" [Wiley 2020].

Connect with Fran

Email: fran@advantages.net

LinkedIn: www.linkedin.com/in/franbidermangross/

Facebook: facebook.com/FranBGross

Instagram: @franbidermangross

Website: www.advantages.net/

Book: "How to Lead a Values-Based Professional Services Firm: 3 Keys to Unlock Purpose and Profit" - Get your copy at https://3keysbook.com/ or on Amazon.

Podcast: "How to Drive Profit with Purpose" - Listen now at www.3keysbook.com/podcast

CHAPTER 3

Embracing Sonder: Finding Meaning in Life's Stories

By Savana Maxon

"You may encounter many defeats, but you must not be defeated. In fact, it may be necessary to encounter the defeats so you can know who you are, what you can rise from, how you can still come out of it."
- Maya Angelou

AS I SIT AT MY DESK, surrounded by knick-knacks, artwork lovingly crafted by my kids and photographs, my eyes are drawn to a sticky note with "Sonder" written in bold letters. It serves as a reminder of the understanding that has become my guiding light - the understanding that every person I encounter has their own unique story, just as complex and important as my own.

It took me years to grasp this concept after struggling in relationships both personally and professionally. A mentor introduced it to me, and it's changed everything. For so long, I found it difficult to trust and truly connect with others. I often ended up in one-sided relationships where I prioritized the needs of others over my own. To cope, I became skilled at wearing different masks, each carefully crafted to hide my inner turmoil. But even as an adult, I still carried the weight of childhood trauma and fear of abandonment with me.

Trust always seemed just out of reach for me - like a fragile thread that would unravel at any moment. As a child, I hid bruises under long sleeves; as an adult, I flinched at unkind words spoken behind closed doors. The question "Will they leave me too?" was constantly on my mind whenever someone showed kindness towards me.

Despite outward success and recognition, I grappled with persistent feelings of inadequacy. Whether through casual remarks from my boss or subtle criticisms from loved ones, self-doubt eroded my sense of worth. As I ascended the ladder of success, I found myself feeling isolated at the peak. The accolades and praise from others were overshadowed by the deafening silence within. Moreover, climbing this ladder of success often came with its own double-edged backlash, as both bosses and spouses, who should have been supportive, instead added weight to my burden.

My need for validation and approval had become a heavy burden, weighing down my spirit and stifling my true self. But in the darkness, a spark of rebellion ignited within me. At a crucial crossroads between conformity and freedom, I made the decision to shape my future and redefine my identity.

As I continue to embrace the concept of "Sonder," I see the world through a new lens - one of empathy and understanding. No longer did I see others as mere background characters in my own story, but rather individuals with their own struggles and experiences. It was liberating to no longer need others for validation for my identity, and instead embrace the complexity of the human experience. This new mindset transformed how I approached people and conflicts, leading me to interact with authenticity and empathy.

Now, I would like to share with you the transformative power of Sonder. By using it as a guide in approaching people and conflicts, we can cultivate authenticity and empathy in all aspects of our lives. This not only sets us free from societal pressures and expectations but also has a ripple effect on those around us, creating stronger connections and understanding between individuals.

Confronting Shadows

Fear was my constant companion from a young age. While most children were learning their ABCs and playing with friends, I was navigating the unpredictable world of substance abuse with my father. His love and charm were overshadowed by his addictions to alcohol and drugs, which often caused him to explode into uncontrollable rage.

I cherished the moments of adventure with my father at his favorite bars as a little girl - an unconventional but special bonding experience for us. We would order Shirley Temples and play on arcade games while the waitresses kept cups of quarters behind the bar just for me. In those moments, I could see my father's warmth and happiness as he had a beer or two with friends or played pool. But as the night went on and the bottles emptied, he would transform into a stranger with glazed eyes. It was like someone had taken over my loving father's body. This drastic shift confused and scared me; I never knew when his mood would change or what would trigger his anger and verbal abuse.

As a child, I couldn't comprehend the complexities of substance abuse. My father's behavior baffled me - why couldn't he just stay sober for me? So, I learned to act a certain way in hopes of avoiding triggering his temper.

His constant belittlement became normal for me, leaving me constantly questioning my self-worth. But every slur and insult only fueled my determination to prove him wrong. Through his lessons in reverse, teaching me how not to behave and treat others, I emerged stronger and more resilient. Though he taught me fear, I chose to lead with empathy and care instead - something he was incapable of.

When my parents decided to finally divorce, I thought it would be an escape from the chaos and toxicity of my home life. Instead, I was left alone every other week to endure my father's unpredictable behavior. But the weeks that I stayed with my mother weren't any better - her new husband was just as abusive, but in a different way. The scent of his cologne continually clung to me; a constant reminder of the predator hidden behind closed doors.

On those dreaded nights, sleep was hard to come by. I would often be jolted awake by a nightmare, but it wasn't the kind that most kids have. There was no way for me to snap out of it; I had to learn how to endure the torment without making a sound until it passed. His presence haunted me long after he left the room, leaving deep scars that could never be erased.

Despite these wounds, I refused to let them define me. Instead, they have become milestones on my journey towards becoming a strong, resilient woman - someone who can lead, mentor, and thrive despite the darkness that once surrounded her.

After the truth of what happened behind closed doors came to light, a lengthy legal battle ensued. I became a ward of the state and went to live with my struggling grandmother. My traumatic childhood left deep emotional wounds that continued to haunt me into adulthood, with no positive role models or guidance. Every challenge felt like trying to walk in oversized shoes. But even though I was battered and broken, I refused to let my past break me.

Looking back on those dark years, I am grateful for the strength and resilience it took to survive. During that time, I was lost and longing for love and acceptance from anyone who would offer it.

But life had one more surprise in store for me - two lines on a pregnancy test that changed everything. Panic overtook me initially, a natural response for someone who has only known instability. Yet, something shifted within me - a fierce protectiveness I never knew existed. This child, my child, would have a different life.

Through her, I found strength not just to endure, but to thrive - even when it meant making mistakes along the way. For her sake, I was determined to create a loving and stable home that was denied to me growing up. I wanted to give her every opportunity possible, no matter how much hard work or sacrifice it required.

In this journey of motherhood, I had to learn not to let fear hold me back or shy away from unfamiliar challenges. Instead, I actively sought opportunities for growth and learning, finding solutions for both clients and colleagues.

As I navigated the unfamiliar territory of raising a child on my own, my daughter and I formed an unbreakable bond. I did everything in my power to provide for her and take on both parental roles, but I couldn't help feeling inadequate and directionless more times than not. I did everything in my power to fulfill both motherly and fatherly roles for her, but as she grew older, I could see the longing in her eyes for a father figure to give her love and validation. It reminded me of my own childhood void.

When I did finally meet someone who seemed to embrace our mother-daughter package, I thought I had found our missing puzzle piece. I rushed into marriage before my daughter's 5th birthday, hoping it would fill the void in both our lives. But it didn't take long, the cracks in our relationship became more visible - constant fighting, manipulation, and doubts creeping in. Despite my desperate desire for a happy marriage, I couldn't shake the feeling that this wasn't true love after all.

Unraveling the Toxic Veil

Sitting in my therapist's office, I nervously fidget with my hands. I had come seeking help and guidance to mend my fractured marriage, which had been worn down by my husband's emotional abuse and past traumas. As we delve into our sessions, they begin to focus more on addressing my own traumas rather than the ongoing and very present communication problems that are preventing us from healing and connection.

My therapist gently suggests exploring the patterns in our arguments, her voice probing into the deepest corners of my psyche. Each argument feels like a jigsaw puzzle with sharp edges that cut deep. My husband's refusal to take responsibility for his actions and his manipulation using my past traumas is all too familiar - it's a never-ending dance that leaves us spinning in circles, unable to move forward.

"Yesterday," I start, my voice steadier than it feels, "we spiraled again." The words taste bitter as they slip out. Shawn and I had been discussing something trivial but then, like a spark to dry tinder, the conversation exploded.

I recount to my therapist how it escalated, how he twisted my words, how he dredged up my history of abandonment, wielding it like a weapon. With each detail, it's as if I'm picking at the edges of a scab, the pain fresh and raw beneath. I'm back in that moment, feeling small and cornered, the air in our living room thick with accusations.

"It's like... with every word he says, the past just claws its way back into the present," I explain, the frustration knotting in my chest. "He knows exactly how to use my history against me, leaving me to defend not only myself but the child I once was, the one who couldn't fight back."

I pause, taking in a deep breath, trying to steady the tremor in my hands. It's hard not to feel defeated when every attempt at peace is met with a renewed assault on my sense of self.

"Does this feel normal to you?" she asks quietly, her question slicing through the noise in my head.

Normal? The word hangs in the air between us, an uninvited guest. My mind races back to countless nights of pillow-muffled tears, to the days where I walked on eggshells, my spirit balancing precariously on the hope that things would change. But they didn't. They haven't.

"Normal" has been a chameleon, blending into whatever chaos surrounds me. But that's the trap, isn't it? Accepting the unacceptable until you can't tell where you end, and the dysfunction begins.

"Normal" is a dance that exhausts, spinning in endless circles, until I'm too weary to notice I'm dancing alone, my partner's steps never quite matching mine.

"Is this normal?" I echo, steadier in my voice. "No, but I am coming to the realization that what I have accepted as 'normal' has hindered my true self and who I aspire to be."

"Then maybe," my therapist offers, understanding in her gaze, "it's time for you to redefine what 'normal' means for you."

In that moment, as the weight of my husband's unacknowledged abuse presses down on me, I realize that the path to finding my true self does not lie in fixing a marriage that is collapsing under its own toxicity.

It lies in having the courage to acknowledge my pain, to hold it up to the light and declare that it has served its purpose - teaching me resilience and creating space for growth.

As I faced the unknown of a new beginning, I grieved for the loss of my familiar discomfort. Fear never left my side, but I learned to embrace it as a necessary part of my journey. Through self-reflection and inner strength, I recognized that the pain I felt was not born from anger towards those who caused it; it came from love - my ability to love - which had been taken for granted and mistreated. This realization weighed heavily on me but also served as a guiding light; it burdened me by choice, yet it also illuminated the path to change once I realized I didn't have to carry it alone.

Weaving Resilience: Crafting a Life of Empowerment

In the bustling atmosphere of the networking event, I felt like an imposter among the chatter and buzz all around in the room of successful professionals. As my colleague, a successful keynote speaker, took the stage with ease and confidence, drawing every eye to her radiant poise, I couldn't help but feel out of place.

She spoke of mentorship and dreams realized and urged us to write down our own dreams on the blank card provided with our dinner plates. I found myself frozen, unable to commit to writing anything.

But as the white card glinted under the soft lighting, it taunted me with its emptiness.

After the event, back at home I sat at my desk feeling frustrated and overwhelmed. As my gaze fell upon a pile of colorful sticky notes, I had an impulse to grab them and retreat to my bedroom with a glass of wine. Instead of writing down my dreams, I wrote down everything I didn't want or refuse to accept in my life any longer. "Settling is not living," I whispered as I filled each note with words like "unworthy" and "insecurity." It was cathartic; each word felt like a piece of baggage I have been carrying.

But amidst all the negative words emerged something surprising - for every dozen negative word, a positive one surfaced from my subconscious. And then it hit me - these were not just words, but chains holding me back.

With each note placed on the bed in front of me, I felt a sense of empowerment and release. No longer was I hiding these parts of myself; instead, I was facing them head-on and stripping them of their power. The room seemed to change around me as I continued to fill the space with words like "valued" and "seen."

As the last note was placed, a flicker of triumph ignited within me. These boundaries were now my craftsmanship, defining the garden of my soul where self-respect blooms in defiant colors. No more shadows, no more silence for the sake of a false peace. I was ready to embrace my worth and live without fear or shame.

I sat in my quiet room, surrounded by sticky notes and the remnants of tear-stained tissues. Each note held a painful truth, a piece of myself that I had buried for far too long.

I remembered the countless sleepless nights spent worrying about others, neglecting my own needs and wants. But now, with each sticky note torn off the wall, I was reclaiming my autonomy and finding empowerment in the act of self-care.

As I reflected on my journey, I recognized the value of setting boundaries and standing up for what I deserved. It wasn't an easy process, but it led me towards a deeper understanding of Sonder - the realization that every individual has their own struggles and stories, and by sharing them, we can create empathy and connection.

I wrote these thoughts down on one final sticky note before placing it in on top of the pile. It served as a reminder to always be intentional in creating the life I wanted, rather than letting life happen to me.

And as I looked around at all the colorful sticky notes, I realized they had become more than just pieces of paper with words scribbled on them. They were symbols of my growth and strength, reminders to never lose sight of who I truly am. And for that, I am grateful.

Fulfillment Through Sonder: Embracing Authenticity and Connection

Sonder has been my guiding force, leading me away from a destructive relationship and towards a fulfilling life. It was through embracing empathy that I found a deeper understanding of myself and the impact I have on those around me. It's not always easy, but by recognizing the shared struggles and journeys we all face, I am able to push through challenges and inspire others to do the same.

Through Sonder, I have not only found personal fulfillment, but also built a successful business helping others incorporate empathy into their businesses, personal lives, and create positive change. As a leader in my community, I have created space for diverse voices to be heard and fostered a sense of belonging.

Balancing these responsibilities while raising four children is no easy feat, but they are also my greatest source of inspiration. Each of them plays a unique role in shaping me into a better person and mother. My eldest's passion for exploration and creativity reminds me to embrace individuality, while my second child's curiosity motivates me to continue learning. My third child's bold spirit challenges me to think outside the box, and my youngest child's unwavering kindness teaches me about compassion every day.

Even with the demands of work, advocacy, and parenthood, I find solace in simple moments with loved ones - shared laughter, comforting hugs, or peaceful movie nights. In these moments, I see the power of Sonder manifesting itself, connecting us all in understanding and unity.

Thanks to Sonder, I was able to open myself up to love when Jacob reentered my life - a constant source of support who believed in my personal growth. Our love may sound like something out of a fairy tale, but it is genuine and deep rooted. His empathy brought us together on a deeper level and continues to support our growth.

As I continue to confront and accept traumas from my past, Jacob stands by me with unwavering support and guidance. Maintaining a healthy relationship takes effort, but his consistent backing gives me the strength to overcome challenges and evolve as an individual. I am endlessly grateful for finding someone who accepts and supports me wholeheartedly.

Fulfilling my commitments to clients, family, and community continues to empower a true sense of purpose and fulfillment - something I was missing for far too long. While embracing Sonder has brought about healing and progress, finding peace with my past without feeling burdened by shame is an ongoing battle. But it serves as a testament to our resilience when we support and empower one another.

Although my journey towards self-discovery is ongoing, I refuse to let my past define me. Instead, I use it as fuel for growth and empower others to do the same. By shedding what no longer serves us and working towards our true selves, we can become the architects of our own stories. So, I invite you to embrace Sonder, confront your obstacles with mentorship, pouring your own thoughts and blockers or aspirations onto sticky notes, or whatever process works best for you, and join me on this journey towards self-acceptance and empowerment.

About the Author

Savana Maxon, current Head of Operations at Lucro Consulting, and the visionary behind Sonder Operations, standing out as a highly skilled leader celebrated for her ingenuity in operational strategies. Since Lucro's inception, Savana has played a crucial role in shaping the company's culture and trajectory, achieving a remarkable 300% revenue surge in its second year of operations.

An advocate for diversity, equity, and inclusion, she serves as the Global Ambassador for Women in Tech and serves on the board of several non-profits dedicated to fostering support and opportunities for current and emerging leaders, exemplifying her unwavering commitment to positive change.

Recognized with honors, including two-time Idaho Business Review Women of the Year Honors, Circle of Excellence Honor, and an Accomplished Under 40 nomination, Savana welcomes connections for mentorship or to leverage her consulting expertise.

Connect with Savana

Email: savana@sonderops.com

LinkedIn: https://www.linkedin.com/in/savanamaxon/

Facebook: https://www.facebook.com/savana.maxon

Instagram: @savana_maxon

CHAPTER 4

Let Her In

By Leah Diteljan

"Each time you ignore feeling an emotion, you send another message of abandonment to your heart."

I don't want you to feel this way.

I don't want to say the wrong thing.

I don't want to look like I am competing with them.

I don't want them to think I'm slutty.

I don't want them to quit.

I don't want them to think I don't like them if I don't go.

I don't want them to judge me.

At the core of each one of these *I don't* statements is GUILT. An emotion women's hearts have a VIP ticket to. Leading with what we don't want is easier than being clear on what we do want, and what we do want is often stated with more ease than what we do need. Being called needy, weak, a bitch, boring, dumb, fat, and ugly are all fears that we, as women, share. And as we get older, the greatest insecurity becomes being invisible.

Guilt used to be a consistent tenant in my body. One that drove decisions I was not proud of and made from fear of remorse or not being liked. I have made some strides in unlearning and dismantling some of these inherited beliefs around guilt, and it has taken tenacity and dedication. Getting to know myself on a very intimate and vulnerable level is something I am committed to in this life. What this level of self-awareness affords is encouraging healing and growth to share more love and connection on this planet. By feeling one emotion at a time and using them as my greatest allies for decision-making, I continue to harmonize my relationship with my intuition and send messages of trust and love to my heart.

My intention for this chapter is to share with you how my relationship with GUILT has become a leading indicator of when I am flexing my tenacious muscles and digging into courageous living when I

Let Her In.

I'll begin with a poem:

Be me
Grow me
Love him and don't let go of loving you
'You' being who you are now
Who is recognizable in the mirror
Who can stare at her infinite potential
and dissipate fear
Who breathes on her own
Without baited breath
And is accepting of all
the universe tests
Breathe in pleasure and your own
divinity
And always keep the promise you made
when you lost yourself
in the patriarchal term,

"virginity"

Redefine your dreams

With him

In them

Feel your soul dance

As he sings to you

On a vulnerable whim

Relinquish his vibrations

Of worship and service

You called this in

It isn't a sin

He's here to help your purpose

When I feel my voice trapped

Grin, and say,

I need you to listen

I can feel his love between my thighs

And anticipate the look in his eyes

As I say his name

In pleasure and pain

Knowing he'll be by my side

I can stop to think

I may need a stiffer drink

To process this gift of resurgent connection

Connectedness

His kingly quality

My highness

Together fear is powerful and limitless

Apart not since before our egos met

Be brave, courageous and unconditional with love

It's in you to give

Your recipient has arrived

So pass him the tools

He can use to build your vessel

Together

So you can float into millions of sunsets forever

Title: Let Him In

I wrote this poem on January 19th, 2020, as it came through me in an unbridled, potent dose of feminine surrender. I was rising in love, (not falling at all) and it couldn't be helped. This poem foreshadowed the relationship I had conjured in my vivid imagination, and it was finally my reality. This poem was an emblem of my empowered voice and became a promise to myself to let him in while continuing to Let Her In (me).

Two weeks later, I flew from Vancouver, Canada, to Sydney, Australia, and shared a week with this man in a small beach town where he grew up. It was the most safe and uncomfortable I had ever felt in someone's presence. I was in awe of his heart, mind, and command of his gentle masculinity. His articulation of the universe and his sincere curiosity about my thoughts and life was intoxicating, and yet I was more conscious than ever before on a "date." He modeled that mirroring the aspects of me that I didn't accept in myself was the greatest gift he could offer me. I was honored to be received with so much love and acceptance. We intimated emotionally, sexually, and intellectually with beautiful French wine, tropical air, and The Revolver album by the Beatles as our soundtrack. This week alchemized the feminine and masculine expression of desire, service, and healing of past circumstances. I flew home with a full heart and promise of seeing each other next month.

The next month never came. The world shut down, and we made one choice—create don't wait. The number one rule of long distance is to book "when" you'll see each other next, and this was out of our control. One conversation at a time, we continued to commit to each other. We wrote two books together that collated the questions we exchanged on Facetime;

we met each other's families on Zoom; we celebrated the birth of my niece; Christmas, Valentine's Day, and our birthdays all virtually for 20 months. This was a moment-to-moment commitment that showed me tenacity isn't a sprint; it's a daily commitment to excruciating patience because of a force beyond that decided long before us: fate.

We were at 15 months of not seeing each other, with no definitive date in sight. I felt guilt consume me for the first time in our relationship as the world began to open in Vancouver instead of Sydney. I gave my phone number to a gentleman that I met poolside. I enjoyed his attention, it felt rejuvenating to be desired LIVE in person again. Since his intentions were unclear and it seemed like a grey area to me, I decided that I would clumsily share this with my boyfriend rather than process guilt in solitude.

"I know I haven't done anything wrong, and yet this feeling of guilt is overwhelming me." The liberation I felt after expressing this and hearing his response was a palpable, expansive sensation in my chest. He lovingly responded by acknowledging that our proximity doesn't have to restrain us from living our physical lives. He said he recognized that he couldn't meet all my sexual needs from Australia and wanted me to go enjoy my body as I chose to. He said he doesn't want to hear about my sexual endeavours, and I can process them with my friends instead. He also requested that the only reason he would want to know anything about my exploration would be if it changed the trajectory of our relationship. When we are together again, we both know that our physical needs will be met, and this clear and impermanent agreement can be explored with privacy.

I felt an extraordinary coursing of love through the cells of my being. This is the true embodiment of freedom and interdependence in a healthy and loving relationship.

After sharing my wonder and awe with a friend, I received a very unexpected and titillating referral to a tantric masseuse. The universe delivered a gift that was infinitely better suited for me than the sundrenched, tattooed biceps that I envisioned poolside. One that was designed entirely for me to receive pleasure and not give any—at all. (Except energetically and, of course, the pleasure of giving in service is a transcendent experience, but not this time from me. Possibly only for the masseuse).

I booked a hotel room, e-transferred my payment, and we met one evening in an exquisite ocean-view suite in downtown Vancouver, with views of the Northshore mountains and the lush rainforest in Stanley Park. I set out candles and diffused patchouli essential oil to open my sacral chakra to receive fully. I opened the door in my white robe, and we began an intimate journey of anticipation and pleasure. We sat on the bed and discussed expectations, important communication cues, and established trust. I openly stated, "If the energy feels aligned for me, I consent for you to enter me." (For those not familiar, a tantric massage moves energy externally and internally based on the recipients' desires. In this case, it was a certified professional, and the only pleasure instrument was hands). We meditated on the bed forehead to forehead, knees to knees, opening our auric fields and welcoming one another's energetic presence. I took my robe off in the candlelight, exposing my naked essence to this immense experience. I whispered softly to myself as I lay on the table, "Body, I love you. You deserve to receive pleasure. You are beautiful." For the next two and a half hours, I relished in my skin, my vitality, my curves, my femininity, my strength, and my attunement to myself. I felt my temperature rise as energy moved through me, beneath my tissue, and ethereally enveloped me. I was impeccably aware of each sensation. I was very aroused. I felt the cells in my body release childhood conditionings of "shoulds" as I exhaled deeper with each breath and melted into the massage table. This table metamorphosized into a throne, which I felt through each respectful graze and gaze in this royal transaction. I was mesmerized by the transference of love and respect this "stranger" offered me without judgment, or reciprocity.

The wonder of what's next, the foreign fingers touching me, this is what my emotional tenacity afforded me that my current conditions could not satiate. I didn't want to have sex with someone else. I wanted my boyfriend, and phone sex wasn't cutting it because the element of physical surprise cannot be replaced with one's own hand. This sensual encounter released suppressed sexual energy and replaced it with consensual stimulation and renewed connection.

It was incredibly self-aware of me to use guilt as an indicator of my unmet needs instead of suppressing it, and it was courageous to express my guilt before it metastasized, as it became a catalyst for a very transformative personal journey. This personal journey reinforced how embracing my relationship with vulnerability empowers me to Let Her In. Every. Single. Time.

I learned that leading with what I need is worth the discomfort of asking. I learned that it's up to me to meet my own needs, and when someone I want to fulfill them can't, continue to use guilt as a guiding compass to navigate toward my desired outcome. In this case, it wasn't an orgasm. In this case (I'll leave the gender of the masseuse to your imagination), the most delicious aspect of this entire expression of guilt-to-satisfaction was me bravely finding a way to meet a need I knew I had. I trusted myself even more than before. I respected myself more than before, and I had alleviated some dense emotions in my cervix from previously unhealthy enmeshments.

What I also learned from the gift of an unexpectedly long long-distance relationship about intimacy and tenacity is emotional agility is attainable with gigantic doses of presence and devotion. These doses must be riddled with sincerity, mature and inexplicable honesty, open-ended curiosity, and tenacious patience.

My invitation to you is to create a list of when you have made decisions out of guilt. How often were they decisions that led with "I don't want…X?" Express what the guilt was trying to tell you instead. Then, create a list with these examples of what you ACTUALLY wanted to do vs what you did to appease others. This list will reveal patterns in your behavior that are quieting you. By identifying what motivated you to make these decisions and then looking back and saying what you want to happen, you are revealing ways you can make changes to create more fulfillment in your life. These changes will Let YOU In.

"Let Her In" is an excerpt from my book "Heal Leah," a personal journey of coming home to myself. Due to be published in 2024.

About the Author

With 16 years of expertise, Leah Diteljan is a transformative executive coach and retreat facilitator, specializing in guiding entrepreneurs within YPO, WPO, and EO toward profound emotional growth. Witnessing the highs and lows of leadership across six continents and 30+ countries, Leah understands the unique challenges faced by high achievers, from multimillion-dollar successes to personal struggles like bullying and divorce.

Her retreats and coaching experiences foster deep connections among leaders, transcending professional success to embrace authentic relationships. Leah's commitment to ongoing learning inspires clients to embark on their own paths of growth. Connect with Leah on LinkedIn for your MindSpa journey:

Connect with Leah

LinkedIn: https://www.linkedin.com/in/leahditeljan/

Facebook: https://www.facebook.com/leah.diteljan

Website: https://mindspamovement.com/

CHAPTER 5

Bet on Yourself and Walk Away

By Pam Howland

I OWN MY OWN EMPLOYMENT law firm and have been practicing law in Idaho for nearly twenty-four years. I am happily married with three kids, all of whom have either reached adulthood or are rapidly approaching it. I have a thriving, fast-paced career where my days are never boring. As anyone in the employment law arena can tell you, this is a profession where there is no shortage of juicy facts and interesting storylines. Unlawful terminations. Harassment. Discrimination. Workplace romance. Exciting!

As I look back now, the path that led me to my law school adventure, and the subsequent events that led me to start my own employment law firm, required tenacity! Along the way there have been numerous failures, countless setbacks, and events that unfolded in ways I could have never anticipated nor predicted. Some of these events were painful. Some were uncomfortable. But I can now see they were all part of the path I had to follow in order to understand what makes me happy and what type of career was going to get me to that place.

Thinking back to December 1996, my path forward looked uncertain, to say the least. My fiancé had broken up with me unexpectedly several months before. And I don't mean an amiable break-up where both parties realize the relationship is not going to work and part ways, wishing each other the best. I mean the type of break-up where you come home from work on the day you have your engagement photos taken, only to find a note that says your fiancé is in love with someone else. Ouch.

On top of that, I was burned out from my sales job selling electronic signs. You may be wondering how I came to be selling signs in the first place. Good question. It probably comes as no surprise that, as a marketing major, I had never aspired to work in the sign business. However, when I graduated from college and found myself needing a job, I ran across a posting in the

Spokane Spokesman Review classifieds advertising for an entry-level marketing major to sell signs. Being that this was the only job posting I appeared to be qualified for, I decided to give it a shot. Four years later, I found my sales skills were actually quite promising—I had met and exceeded my sales goals, and I frequently received large bonuses when I closed substantial sales. However, I had become disenfranchised with the product I was selling. Technology was quickly rendering it obsolete. On top of that, my office was located in a dreary post-World War II industrial park located ten miles outside of the city. Single and sporting a lackluster job, I felt confused and without a purpose as my twenty-seventh birthday rapidly approached. Surely, there was a more challenging career out there than the one I had fallen into?

As I headed into New Year's Eve 1996, the signs were clear: I needed a change. I was beginning to realize that the break-up with my ex-boyfriend had been for the best. And, I had come to realize that the relationship had resulted in some unintended consequences—a potentially interesting new career path for me to follow. My former boyfriend had been attending law school for the majority of our relationship (breaking up with me shortly after his graduation) and as I followed along behind the scenes,

I had become fascinated with the law. It took a New Year's Eve lunch with my mother to push me on the path forward. "If you want to be a lawyer," she said, "then quit complaining about it, apply to law school, and make it happen!"

I took my mother's advice. I bet on myself and walked away from my dissatisfying career selling signs. I worked hard and gave law school everything I had—I was not taking any chances that I would be sent back to the Industrial Park. I got a job during law school working at the U.S. Attorney's office—a fast-paced office with attorneys who tried some of the most high-profile federal cases in the area. I took the classroom work seriously and finished first in my class. I did not just want to become any lawyer—I wanted to become a litigator. And when I say that, I mean I wanted to go to court, I wanted to try cases, and I wanted to spend my time convincing judges and juries why my side should win. I wanted to be like Jack McCoy from Law and Order! I was excited. I was challenged. I felt motivated and unstoppable. I was on fire.

As I entered the legal market, I knew I wanted to go to court. I went straight to the top, securing a job at the Idaho Supreme Court, working for a judge. What better way to learn about getting into the courthouse than by learning from a judge? But where to go next? There were so many options. Perhaps the prosecutor's office? Perhaps in-house for a corporation? Perhaps private practice? This was an exciting time of my life—so many options and so many potential roads to go down that would result in very different outcomes.

Several mentors pointed me in the direction of private civil practice. With my law school transcript in hand, and with tales of my recently-completed clerkship, I was able to secure a job at one of the most prestigious law firms in town—a large regional firm. It was at this firm where I really learned how to be a lawyer. I had amazing mentors and worked on complex cases. I worked alongside attorneys I grew to trust and respect, and I learned how to push a lawsuit through the system from start to finish—a process that takes a long time. I worked with some of the best trial attorneys in the state, and they showed me how to bust through the courthouse doors. I made partner at the regional firm after about a decade of working there. For a brief moment in time, I thought I had arrived to where I was supposed to be. Partnership at a prestigious law firm! Surely, this is what every lawyer wants to achieve?

Several things happened not long after I made partner that changed this perspective and suggested that the universe had other plans for me. One issue involved a changing focus and philosophy within the firm and escalating conflict among various partners. Several of the litigators I was closest to, and who had mentored me throughout the years, abruptly left the firm. About that same time, the firm made the decision to discontinue handling many of the types of cases that I had devoted nearly a decade of time to working on. My mentors were gone. My workload was dwindling. I felt disconnected and I couldn't help but wonder how I ended up in a partnership where I had nothing in common with many of my partners. I felt lonely and isolated. I had few cases and became relegated, somewhat, to a support role helping other attorneys to run their cases.

About this same time, I recall walking through downtown Boise one day and running into a much younger attorney I knew. I was probably ten years older than him, and several years before, while he was still in law school, he had worked as an intern at my law firm. I had supervised him on a couple of matters and had gotten to know him. He greeted me on the street—he had just made an argument to the Idaho Supreme Court. He told me that this was the third argument he had made before the highest court in the state—he was excited. He was out there! He was shaping the law! I was somewhat taken aback by this. Although I had worked at the Supreme Court many years before, I had never returned to argue a case there. And, while some of the cases I had worked on ended up on appeal before the court, other attorneys at my firm were always selected to make the argument. In fact, the reality is that at this point in my career, I was not getting into court at all. Instead, I spent my days typing away at my desk, primarily writing briefs. It hit me at that moment: My career was passing me by. What had I done wrong? Why wasn't I going to court? Why was I getting such unfulfilling assignments, and why were all of the best assignments going to others?

Another thing that happened during that time period involved my then five-year-old daughter, Kennedy. One morning in the Fall of her kindergarten year of school, I volunteered in her classroom. Kindergarten had not gotten off to a great start—she had been wetting the bed every night for over a month and seemed tired and exhausted. As I discussed my observations with her teacher, and as we both compared our observations, we soon came to realize that this seemed like something more than just a difficult transition period—it seemed like it could involve a serious health issue. I rushed Kennedy off to her pediatrician that very day, and within hours, she was diagnosed with Type 1 Diabetes, a somewhat terrifying (and extremely difficult to manage) chronic disease. A person diagnosed with Type 1 is no longer able to produce insulin (a hormone needed to survive), which means that they either get injections of insulin throughout the day or utilize an insulin pump to inject the insulin into them. There really is no other option—if you do not take insulin, you die. If you have ever known someone with Type 1, then you likely understand that it is extremely difficult to manage, and with little kids (such as a five-year-old child), they can go from being just fine one minute to experiencing life-endangering blood sugar lows (or highs) the next. One of my worst memories from those early days of Kennedy's diagnosis is her fear of the continual parade of shots and of having to, at times, pin her down to dose her with insulin. Seeing a look of total fear on your little girl's face as you try to keep her alive is a horrifying thing to deal with, and as anyone who has dealt with Type 1 Diabetes knows, you have to be tenacious to make it through those early years of a young child's diagnosis.

As I struggled to accept my daughter's medical condition and as my family worked to change the way we functioned, the law firm's billable hour requirement (and the pressure that went along with it) became unmanageable. The firm operated a flex-time program, which I opted to participate in, but at least during that time period, the firm had not yet figured out how to make this program a success. Secretly, other women partners warned me, "Do not participate in the reduced-hours program: It will be the kiss of death for your status at the firm." I opted to give the program a shot—I knew I could not hit the higher billable requirement I was required to make. Ultimately, the women who had warned me were right. When the true focus of a law firm is on profitability aimed at achieving high billable hours, there is little room for attorneys who seek to bill less than their peers.

During this time period, although I may have appeared to have achieved success to the outside world, the reality was that I was miserable. I felt undervalued, and I was not getting the type of cases I wanted to work on. I had reached a career dead-end. I was no longer learning and growing, and despite my firm's claim that it valued working mothers who worked reduced-hour schedules, I felt like the billable hour was the only measure of true value for big law. I felt like a failure. I worried about my daughter all day, every day, and I was resentful that I needed to be on site at the firm when my daughter needed me more. While the firm had taught me the skills I needed to practice law, during my last few years there, it had, on many levels, stripped my confidence away. I eventually came to realize that my career, my family, and my mental health all hinged on my ability to walk away and bet on myself.

On a cold winter day in February 2016, I walked out the door of my big firm law office and took a gamble on myself, hanging a shingle and working out of a home office while I got my own start-up law firm up and running. I cannot compare my early years of running my own law firm to anything else I have ever experienced. Every client who called me was a victory. Every case that came through my door was a win. I dropped my kids off in the morning and picked them up after school. Guilt free. I worked at my home office with my kitten on my lap and my dog on the floor beside me. Happiness. I remember the first check I received made payable to my own law firm, and I will never forget the first client who took a chance on me. My career was on the road to recovery. My confidence was starting to come back.

Since then, my firm has grown and changed, but one thing has stayed the same: We do everything we can to set ourselves apart from the typical law culture that dominates our field. While the attorneys at my firm still are required to bill hours, we pride ourselves on operating differently than most traditional law firms, and we do everything we can to make sure the mark of our success does not hinge on the number of hours we bill every year. We make sure our personal lives get the attention they need. And we focus on our relationships with each other—if the people within the office do not feel connected, everything starts to unravel. We truly try to think outside of the box—how can we offer legal services in a way better than everyone else and in a way that gives our clients what they need? What can we do that no other law firm is doing?

What I have learned since my sign-selling days is this: As professionals and as leaders, we grow and change. What works for you one year, and what makes you feel satisfied then, may not work for you the next. This does not mean you failed. It merely means your path is evolving.

Taking chances and embracing change, especially in something as significant as your professional career, can be extremely uncomfortable. However, the upside is great. Those milestone moments in my career—including my decision to go to law school and my decision to start my own law firm—have resulted in opportunities I never imagined were possible. It would have been easy to maintain the status quo, but the tenacity it took to accept the risk, bet on myself, and walk away when the time was right paid off.

About the Author

Pam Howland has been litigating cases in Idaho state and federal courts since 2001 and has represented employers from around the country against claims encompassing a variety of employment laws, including claims of discrimination, harassment, non-compete violations, trade secret misappropriation, wrongful termination, FLSA, FMLA and ADA. She regularly counsels employers on how to avoid litigation on topics related to discipline, termination, retaliation, internal policies and procedures, and evolving (and complex) laws such as Title VII, the ADA, the FMLA and unfair competition. In February 2016, Pam formed Idaho Employment Lawyers, a boutique law firm dedicated to handling Idaho employment law issues.

In 2023, Pam created Law for Leaders, a training program aimed at keeping business owners, HR professionals, and supervisors, out of the courthouse. Pam also obtained her Global Speaker Certification in 2023 and enjoys speaking to business leaders about her experiences as a litigator and about why they need training to stay out of trouble.

Pam is active in the local community. She currently serves on the Board for the Wassmuth Center for Human Rights and on the Board for Entrepreneur's Organization of Idaho.

HONORS AND AWARDS

- Global Speaker Certification (2023)

- *Idaho Business Review*, Women of the Year (2023)

- *Chambers USA: America's Leading Lawyers for Business*, Labor & Employment (2015, 2023)

- Mountain States Super Lawyers, Top 50 Women Lawyers (2016, 2017, 2023)

- Mountain States Super Lawyers, General Litigation (2013-2015, 2017, 2018, 2019, 2020, 2021, 2022)

- Idaho State Bar Service Award 2020

- Idaho State Bar Professionalism Award 2021

- *Idaho Business Review,* Accomplished Under 40 Award (2009)

- *Idaho Business Review,* Leaders in the Law (2016)

EDUCATION

GONZAGA UNIVERSITY SCHOOL OF LAW, J.D., *summa cum laude,* May 2000

MONTANA STATE UNIVERSITY, Bachelor of Science in Business, 1993

Empower Your Business with Pam's Expertise: Take proactive steps to protect your business and empower your leadership! Visit www.lawforleaders.com to learn about how her training program can keep your organization out of legal trouble. Visit www.idemploymentlawyers.com to learn more about her employment law practice and services.

Connect with Pam

Email: phowland@idemploymentlawyers.com

LinkedIn: https://www.linkedin.com/in/pamsimmonshowland/

Facebook:
https://www.facebook.com/Idahoemploymentlawyers/

Instagram: @idemploymentlawyers

CHAPTER 6

Too Much Tenacity?

By Andrea Herrera

IN THIS ANTHOLOGY, you'll encounter the powerful voices of women whose stories are monuments to tenacity—a force that has shaped their journeys through the rugged terrains of entrepreneurship. My own story weaves into this rich tapestry, rooted in a heritage of resilience and an unwavering spirit to overcome.

From my grandfather, a prizefighter whose every punch was a testament to his grit, to my parents, who navigated life's adversities with unparalleled perseverance, tenacity is my inheritance. Their stories, distinct yet intertwined, laid the foundation for my own path, teaching me that resilience in the face of adversity is not just a trait but a choice—a choice to push forward, to dream big, and to carve out a path that honors those who came before us.

My father's journey, from selling flowers in the subway at the age of 5, living in a one-room tenement with his family of five and no bathroom or running water in the room, through a myriad of other challenges. His ultimate embrace of entrepreneurship illuminated the transformative power of determination. Meanwhile, my mother's quest for freedom from a conservative upbringing in a very strict and traditional home in the suburbs led her to the heart of Chicago's Old Town in the 1960s, where she immersed herself in the era's folk music and counterculture. She sought a life beyond the conventional and she flourished by doing so.

Their marriage, although brief, was comprised of hopes, dreams, and challenges and was a lesson in resilience. Navigating sexism, racism, and other societal barriers, they remained lifelong friends, their bond a testament to mutual respect and understanding.

Expanding Horizons Through Education
and Experience

Inspired by my parents' reverence for education, travel, and experiences, my upbringing was rich with opportunities for learning and exploration. College was not just an aspiration; it was a given. There, leadership roles beckoned, each experience laying another stone on my path. Post-graduation, the corporate world offered a decade of valuable lessons while it also revealed a misalignment with my deeper aspirations. This realization prompted a bold decision—to leave the security of a corporate job and embark on a cross-country motorcycle journey, seeking clarity and purpose. It was a pivotal moment, marking the start of my entrepreneurial journey with Amazing Edibles.

The Birth of Amazing Edibles and Lessons
in Resilience

Starting Amazing Edibles was a leap into the unknown—a venture begun with audacity but without a formal business plan. The early years were a testament to hard work and the support of my community, especially as I navigated the challenges of being a new mother and a business owner. Yet, it was during times of crisis, such as the aftermath of 9/11 and the Great Recession of 2008, that my tenacity was truly tested. Each crisis decreased our revenue by over 50% overnight and demanded innovation and adaptability, pushing me to find new ways to sustain and grow my business.

A Journey Through Grief and Resilience

Tenacity has its limits. The pandemic of 2020 was perhaps our greatest challenge, forcing us to pivot dramatically in response to a world transformed overnight. Through it all, we remained committed to our community, our vision, and the belief that tenacity, when channeled with purpose and compassion, can overcome the most daunting obstacles. Our business became almost illegal overnight. We laid off 80% of our team; it was the worst day in our company's history. The challenges of the pandemic were many. Revenue was down 80% when offices, schools, and community spaces were all declared closed and off-limits. We could not cater food, as nobody was there to eat it. We could not create amazing celebrations, as they were outlawed in Chicago, one of the most regulated cities in the country during the pandemic. We then pivoted immediately to home delivery service with a hardworking and passionate crew. A few months later, we created a "luxury connection gift box" that became a major pivot in our business model and got us through the first year of the pandemic. While facing professional uncertainty on a daily basis, I also experienced incredible loss. In the course of 6 months, in the fall of 2022, I lost my mother very quickly from a fatal side effect of medication in a clinical trial. She was at dinner with her best friend Wednesday evening, and Monday morning, we were forced to end life support. Then, just two weeks later, a dear friend died. Work went on, and we made it through the holiday season. We hunkered down to hibernate for another winter in Chicago during the Pandemic, and when spring came, four more friends and family members died, one each week for four weeks in April. And it was the personal losses that brought me to the brink. The cumulative weight of complicated grief and the constant battle to keep the business afloat tested my resilience like never before. It was a dark period, marked by moments of despair, including excessive drinking, anxiety, depression, and a grappling with my identity. Who was I if my company failed? When would the pandemic, and the pain, end?

Seeking Help and Embracing Self-Care

The turning point came one late afternoon on the rooftop of my apartment building, 35 stories up. I went up to enjoy a cocktail after work at sunset, and the depth of my despair became frighteningly clear. I looked out over the city I loved and felt I did not have the strength to go on. It was a moment of reckoning. In a flash, my son, Jake, came to my mind and heart, leading me off the rooftop to seek help and to finally prioritize my well-being. I learned that tenacity is not just about enduring but also about knowing when to pause and when to seek support.

The months that followed were a time of healing and introspection. I embraced therapy, meditation, medication, and rest. Long walks on the beach and a two-month sabbatical from work. I finally started to recognize that the tenacity I prized needed to be applied to self-care. This period of slowing down was not just about recovery but about rediscovering my purpose and redefining my approach to business and life.

Reflections on Tenacity, Resilience, and the Power of Vulnerability

As I reflect on my journey, I see a tapestry woven with threads of tenacity, resilience, and the courage to be vulnerable. The challenges I faced, both personal and professional, taught me invaluable lessons about the strength that comes from embracing one's vulnerabilities and that prioritizing self-care, even if that means slowing down, is a critical piece in the pursuit of tenacity.

Empowering Others Through Shared Stories of Resilience

By sharing my story, I hope to inspire others who may find themselves facing similar challenges. It is a reminder that true tenacity is not just about fighting to overcome obstacles but about having the courage to confront our vulnerabilities, to seek help when needed, and to prioritize our well-being alongside our ambitions.

This collection of stories is a tribute to the spirit of tenacity that drives us to dream, to strive, and to overcome. It is a celebration of the resilience that enables us to face adversity with courage and to emerge stronger, wiser, and more determined than ever. May these stories inspire you to embrace your challenges with tenacity, to care for yourself with the same fervor with which you pursue your dreams, and to remember that sometimes, the most courageous act is to pause, reassess, and nurture your spirit on the path to achieving your goals.

Please feel welcome to reach out and connect via LinkedIn.

About the Author

Andrea Herrera is founder and president of Amazing Edibles Catering, an award winning catering company that fosters relationship building at bread breaking events. She is proud of the amazing team assembled who live by our core values of Hard Working, Problem Solving, Thoughtful, and Team. Her personal mission is to Foster Connection to Create Community. She has served over a million meals in Chicago in the past 30 years.

In April of 2020 due to the Pandemic Andrea realized a quick pivot was necessary as her legacy catering company would likely need to hibernate till events started happening again. So she thought about her talents, values and her resources and sought to find an answer to a problem in the world, thus was born Boxperience. Boxperience solves the challenge of connecting with top clients in a world where lunches and dinners are no longer the go to connection event. With Boxperience we deliver an amazing invitation to a shared experience over food and drink in a customized gift box.

Andrea is a proud global leader, the past Champion for Women of EO in The Entrepreneurs Organization, a global organization of 20,000 members currently serving on the global leadership committee, past positions include president of Chicago chapter of EO, Chair of the Accelerator program to mentor emerging entrepreneurs, and chair of a global conference on entrepreneurial leadership in 2016. Andrea was just selected as one of the top 100 Titans of Industry for Chicago in 2024. She is the proud mother of Jake Hoover, her greatest achievement. She has also served on the boards of Cornell College, Global Citizenship Experience HS, A Children's Place, and as past chair of the board of Rivendell Theatre Ensemble – a theatre dedicated to advancing the lives of women through theatre. Andrea has been profiled in Hispanic Living magazine, CNN Money, MSNBC, Chicago Tribune, Today's Chicago Woman and in the book From Risk to Reward profiling her entrepreneurial journey. Last year she hit 5 continents and looks forward to completing all 7. One favorite client, Oprah Winfrey, loved our grilled veggies! Amazing Edibles supports numerous local charities and not for profits that focus on and support women and children with in kind donations totaling 5% of annual revenue.

Connect with Andrea

Email: andrea@amazingediblescatering.com

LinkedIn: https://www.linkedin.com/in/andreaherreraamazingedibles

Facebook: https://www.facebook.com/andrea.herrera.39

CHAPTER 7

Tenacity in the Face
of the Unknown

By Dr. Kristin L. Kahle

HERE I AM WRITING this chapter at the Borealis base camp in
Alaska, looking at the beautiful scenery out the window and
having a great glass of champagne. After seeing the Northern
lights last night and playing with some Alaskan dogs and puppies
this morning, I sat down to write my chapter. My company,
NavigateHCR, was sold to a private equity company, of which I
have an extension of a contract (from five years originally to
another five years). The team is in its busy season, and I am
getting few emails from them about any issues. I feel like I finally
have the best team and things are going extremely well as
compared to the uphill battle I had growing this company for

the past 10 years. This is the first time that I feel like I can breathe and have a clear path for all who work with me.

When I first formed NavigateHCR, I started it as a service-based company with the intention of selling it in a few years after reaching profitability. NavigateHCR was really formed to be an Affordable Care Act compliance company. The first year we planned to transmit ACA data to the government, but the government was not yet set up to receive any transmissions of data. So, this caused me to make some shifts in the business; we had sold clients on the basis that the government wanted this first year of filing and we had staff in place to do this. This was probably the darkest time for the business: relying on being a government vendor and the government moves the deadline— you still have to run a business. This was one of the only times that I had to max out my credit cards to make payroll and take a loan that I was not sure I could pay back to survive a full year. Because of this change, I also had to create additional products that would bring in more revenue in order to survive the year if the government wanted to make any other changes.

I had a one-year line of credit, one year of maxed-out credit cards, and one year to figure out how to bring in more revenue and more clients. I love the quote "sales cure all ails," so that is what I had to do: really crack down and become a selling machine. I had debt, had the team, and had the clients; now I needed the revenue. However I did not have a true solution other than some great spreadsheets to resolve the need for clients so they may look at data differently in a new way. The data for reporting at that time was going to be an issue, so I needed to resolve that for the clients and provide a different solution. With my back against the wall and with all the negativity and self-doubts in my head, I decided it was time for me to create my own software to answer the issues that our clients were having. Why did I think I could create and sell software? Looking back on this now, I think I was over-ambitious to think that in one year, I could do both.

Now that I was determined to be a founder and CEO of a software company, I went running out to Barnes and Noble to find a *Software Company for Dummies* book. Well, it does not exist, so my maxed-out credit cards allowed me enough to purchase four books to understand how to create and run a software company. All of these books were way over my head. I had no idea what they were talking about; new words, new logic, and lots of coding conversations. So I would work all day running the company, selling products to clients, and then do my school work (finishing up my Doctorate degree) and study about software companies and how to run them after hours. I felt completely out of my comfort zone and was questioning every move, like what do I know about running a software company?

That itty bitty shitty committee in my head was really trying to take me down and out. I decided to give in to it and hand off the software project to someone else who convinced me that they were capable and able to do this kind of project. I decided that the best use of my time and talents was to stay in the sales swim lane and let the project manager manage the software project. I set off for weekly update meetings and weekly technology and software brainstorming with a firm date from the government that year in order to have a product to market by then. If the project manager had been able to come to a fusion with the software product, I might have a different story to tell. But here is the down and dirty (and quick recap) of what happened: The company we hired could not deliver, my credit cards were once again maxed out, the line of credit was gone and could not get more, the project manager could not deliver on anything, and we now had 60 days to finish before the deadline. I did not mention this, but I was selling like crazy (or selling like hot cakes) and had several clients that were looking for us to deliver, and we had no software product to speak of. So, shoot, what do I do now? How do I not let down clients or employees when I have nothing to deliver to them?

Feeling like I completely caused this chain of events, I had to come up with a solution that could meet this deadline. We were back to where we started and lost all the time that we just spent on creating a failure of a software system. Now I know that most software on the first round does not make it to market, but then I thought how am I the only one that cannot get this to market? Am I not smart enough? Not talented enough? Do I not have enough grit? What am I missing? I turned into a crazy person to get this done; this was a person I had not seen before, nor do I want to see again. I completely became a control freak and was trying to hold everything close to the vest. Understanding that is not good for the growth of the team or the growth of myself as a leader, I decided to figure out how I could manage this without micromanaging all these items.

Here are some of the steps that I took:

1. Define the project scope. Narrowing it down to achievable tasks and actions that would be deployed.

2. Define swim lanes. Looking at the team, who is responsible for what and how they are measured on those items. Looking at tactical items that would be accomplished as well.

3. Hold accountability meetings. Holding daily stand-up meetings with a clear countdown of the days and how much time is left.

4. Keep sketches of software and have a whiteboard of software flow, so when I had a thought, an idea, or a flash in the middle of the night, I could capture it.

On top of that great game plan, I wish I could tell you that it worked. It did not work. One of my favorite lines to remember is that there are 26 letters in the alphabet, and if Plan A does not work out, you have more letters to pick from. So, with very few days left to deliver and another plan in the trash, we moved to the best possible route, and that was to use a little duct tape. Taking some software that was off the shelves, hiring some macro and pivot table writers, and deploying staff over 24 hours a day, we hit that deadline and successfully filed for our first round of clients. But wow, many lessons were learned from that experience.

After that experience and some self-reflection, I looked at what was best for me and my growth as a CEO and founder and the current team we had in place. One thing was clear: The team and the partner that was involved needed to shift. Making some dramatic moves, the partner was out of the business, along with some of the team who were not on board to have a start-up mentality, whose positions were eliminated. Now was the time to focus on the software. I decided to bring that in-house and run the team myself. Still looking for that Dummies book for software founders, I decided to write my own book and come up with a way to deploy projects. What I ultimately struggled with was the developers and their meeting (or not meeting) all the deadlines, which in turn is an avalanche of dates that must move if those are not accomplished. I decided to create my own job project board and post it for all software projects. Came up with a way to make this more of a project scope. Some of my steps are listed below:

1. Created the software project, naming it and gave it a number (so we can track it).

2. Created the script of what it should look like.

3. Create the data flow: where does the data need to go, and what does the data need to do.

4. Create a bench of software developers that can bid on these projects.

5. Allow the software developer to come up with a timeline according to all the items that are given to them.

6. If they achieve that timeline, with delivery in advance of the initial timeline, they will get a monetary bonus. However, if they do not achieve the date, then a monetary decrease in the project scope will occur.

7. Grading all the developers after their projects are completed based on how active and bug-free their projects are submitted.

8. Grading all developers based on the core values of the company.

9. Creating a bench of developers to give them the next round of projects.

10. Creating a way to track each project and each developer and creating software to do this.

Now that I had a true game plan with development, I was thinking what could go wrong? As I have learned some valuable lessons, it is not that things can go wrong; it is that I should be asking the question, how can we do better? We have a truly busy season, and with that busy season, we are always deploying new software (deploying software every week). At the end of that season, I am always asking the question, what can we do better? What will help my team be more effective? What are clients looking for that we do not have? What can I, as a leader, do better? What else does my team need from me as a leader? Who are the next leaders in the company? I truly believe that leaders ask questions, and I always want to be asking the questions and coming up with the solutions that the team and clients need.

Now that I have been running a software company for over 10 years, I am looked at as a forward thinker in software development. If you had asked me years ago, "Where do you see yourself?," it would have never been in software development. Knowing that I do not have a background in this, I always thought that I could not learn something this challenging and new in my life. This chapter is really dedicated to those people out there who want to break away from what they know and start something new and take that leap of faith. Remember to shoot for the moon because, even if you miss, you may land among the stars.

About the Author

Meet Dr. Kristin L. Kahle, also known as Dr. K. (because let's face it, she sounds like a rapper), the wizard of simplifying business with a touch of fun! By day, she's your tech-savvy sidekick, untangling those knotty business processes. But when the sun sets, she's on a mission to share her wisdom, especially with the awesome women in business!

Now, let's talk about her nerdy side - and she's proud of it! Dr. K. is a certified genius, boasting a lineup of degrees taller than a skyscraper. She's got a Certified Healthcare Reform Specialist badge, a Doctor of Business Administration (DBA) from Argosy University, a Master of Business Administration (MBA) from the University of Phoenix, and a Bachelor of Arts (BA) from Pine Manor College.

But here's the real kicker: Dr. K. isn't just about the degrees. Nope, she's also a bestselling author with four incredible books under her belt. Ever heard of "Crash and Learn"? It's where she spills the beans on epic failures and bouncing back stronger than ever. And in "Notivation," she's all about the power of saying "No" (with a big dose of humor) to make those million-dollar dreams a reality.

Some other of her adventures in the business world can be read on the pages of "Lead Like a Woman: Tales from the trenches" and "Lead Like a Woman: Audacity". A compilation of stories where successful women share their stories about learning, leading, and achieving goals.

Oh, did I mention she's a media superstar too? You'll find her popping up in all the coolest magazines, from The CIO Today to CEO Weekly, chatting about innovation and cheering on fellow women in business. Plus, The Global BIZ Outlook named her one of the Top Transformational Leaders of 2023 - how awesome is that?

And wait, there's more! Dr. K. is the fearless leader of Navigate HCR, a powerhouse company she founded. With a dream team of specialists, they assist brokers, employers, team leaders, and companies on everything HR compliance, healthcare law, ACA, and more legislative developments.

So, whether she's coaching entrepreneurs, gracing magazine covers, or leading Navigate HCR, Dr. Kristin L. Kahle - aka Dr. K. - is all about making business exciting, empowering, and downright awesome!

Connect with Kristin

Email: drk@navigatehcr.com

LinkedIn: https://www.linkedin.com/in/drkristinkahle/

https://www.linkedin.com/company/doctork/

Facebook: https://www.facebook.com/drkkahle

X: @TheDoctorKK

Web: https://drkristinkahle.com/

CHAPTER 8

Breakthrough After
the Breakdown

By Cathey Kuo

"THE BREAKTHROUGH COMES AFTER THE BREAKDOWN" is something I have been saying quite often recently to both friends and podcast guests as I personally experienced the breakdown recently and am now living the breakthrough.

When I Googled the definition of tenacity, the first thing I got, from Vocabulary.com, was: "someone who just won't quit—who keeps trying until they reach their goal" whereas Merriam-Webster defines tenacious as: "persistent in maintaining, adhering to, or seeking something valued or desired."

During the "breakdown" phase of my journey, I did not believe I was the least bit tenacious, so if you are there, I want you to know there is hope and there is a light at the end of it all. Please have faith, and please don't ever give up on your dreams, goals, or yourself.

I was severely depressed for almost 8 months of my life last year and could barely get out of bed most days. I would go to do Hot Yoga or Hot Pilates early in the morning, but after coming home and showering, I would slip back into bed and just meditate for two or three hours unless I had a meeting I could not miss. This was my routine for almost eight months of my life. I would do the bare minimum in my business and life as I felt I had lost my purpose and, in turn, my drive and the fire that fueled me. After over three decades of being a high achiever, hustler, and always doing all the things nonstop, I finally hit a wall. Luckily, I had built my businesses up to a point where they were on autopilot to an extent, and I have both an amazing business partner and life partner (separate people) who helped keep things afloat. That, paired with my healthy savings and investments, allowed me the freedom to experience the depression or, as I like to call it now, my spiritual sabbatical, without too much damage.

At 34 years old, it was the first time in my entire life that I ever experienced severe anxiety or depression. Maybe I'm lucky that it didn't hit me till so late in life as I had often heard people describe the symptoms but could never quite empathize or understand until I finally experienced and lived it myself. Also, now that I have experienced it, I am so grateful for so many reasons. Firstly, it allows me to empathize genuinely with those who currently are or have in the past experienced crippling anxiety or depression. Second, it helps me appreciate even more the joy, love, happy days, and good times now that I know what it is like to not feel this way.

Prior to this experience, my baseline for the majority of my adult life was happy and joyful as I had worked a lot on personal development to get there after a somewhat challenging upbringing as the child of first-generation immigrants. Nothing too crazy, just the normal challenges of assimilating and building a life in America after my parents had come to this country with nothing and had to start from zero and build up from there.

As the child of first-generation immigrants, my main purpose in life from the time I was old enough to understand what was going on around me was to achieve financial freedom and financial security for my parents #1 and then for myself #2. While we were fortunate enough to always have food to eat, clean water to drink, and a roof over our heads while I was growing up, we lived frugally as we had just enough to get by somewhat comfortably, albeit sometimes it was the bare minimum like $1 frozen pizzas and TV dinners or instant ramen as I had mentioned previously in my chapter in *Lead Like a Woman: Audacity*. The ironic part of this story is that when I achieved that goal of financial freedom and security was also when I felt I lost my purpose and slid into a depression. In hindsight, it seems to have been a mix of burnout and conquering my first mountain.

All my life, I had been grinding and hustling to achieve this goal for my family and myself. By 33 years old, I made the most money I had ever made in a single year. I had a great, diversified investment portfolio and healthy savings. My mother and our family real estate investment portfolio were doing great and she could finally retire comfortably if she chose to (she didn't, of course, because she would be bored). Essentially, I had achieved what I thought was my purpose in life and no longer had direction anymore.

Luckily, the universe always has a way of giving you exactly what you need. As such, during this existential crisis, I bumped into a highly successful friend of mine and explained what I was feeling. How I felt I had lost my purpose, how I felt money alone no longer motivated me when that was my main motivator and driving force for years, how I felt I needed to figure out my bigger purpose to reignite my fire, and how I wanted to focus on something that made a greater impact. Something that goes beyond just me and my family. Something that would feel fulfilling in my heart and to my core. I asked questions like, "How can I serve in a greater capacity?" "How can I add value in a greater way?" and "What is the legacy that I would want to leave?"

This friend of mine, Juanny Romero, who is a total badass boss babe and owns multiple coffee shops as well as her own coffee brand and roastery, refers to herself as a creator of community in press interviews as opposed to anything coffee-related when asked what she does. That is why she is as hugely successful as she is as well as a living, prime example of The Second Mountain concept, which is derived from a book she recommended to me during my darkest hours right when I needed it and provided so much clarity about why I was feeling what I was feeling.

From the outside looking in, I should have been ecstatic to be where I was. I seemed like I had it all together on the outside but I was falling apart on the inside. I felt depressed, and there were many days when I wished I wouldn't wake up the next day. Many days when I would just cry for no reason, head in hands wondering what I was supposed to do and begging for clarity and direction because, along with the depression came severe brain fog. It was to the point where I just felt like my brain was broken. I recall telling my EO forum that exact line and explaining how when you break a bone, it is easy to identify and fix, but when you feel like your brain is broken, it is not so easy to identify and fix.

Fast forward a few months later, it was time to immerse myself in Tony Robbins' Date with Destiny, which I had booked over a year prior as I had purchased his mastery bundle when I attended Unleash the Power Within live in Palm Beach and could finally find the time to do it now. This experience and program literally changed my life in the best way possible, and I will be forever grateful for the opportunity. Best money and time

I ever spent, and I am confident the ROI will be more than 100x. Stanford actually did studies on participants, and there was a 100% cure rate for depression, and it certainly cured mine AND reignited my fire. I could probably write a whole book about how and why it helped me achieve this, but for now, I'll share the main breakthroughs I got from the experience.

The first major breakthrough was defining my life mission. As entrepreneurs, so many of us have well-defined mission statements for our business but few ever think through our life mission. He takes you through a process to define your life mission that is much better explained by him than me, so for now, I will just share my experience and results. My life mission is to be a connector, enjoy abundance and growth, and light the way for others. I realized the reason I had achieved the success and goals I had at the age I had is because I am meant to be a connector and light the way for others. I am meant to serve as an inspiration and trailblazer for the child of first-generation immigrants, for the minority women, for the people who are suffering from fear, imposter syndrome, and self-doubt like I was because they didn't see anyone that looked like me where they wanted to be and go.

The second major breakthrough was recognizing my primary question in life, where it stemmed from, how it served me well in the past, why it would no longer serve me in this next phase of life and redefining my new primary question. Essentially, as the child of immigrants, the primary question that I developed from my upbringing was, "How can I help?" as I was always taught to help my parents however, whenever, and wherever I could. At home by helping to cook or clean, with the family business as the executive assistant and doing all the computer-related work, and in their personal lives as a translator when needed since English is their second language.

My first primary question translated to me always wanting to be helpful to people throughout my life, which helped me build an amazing business, community, and circle of friends because of the value I always added to people's businesses and lives. I didn't know it at the time, but I was essentially living The Go Giver concept, another great book that another dear friend recommended to me. By doing this, I became known as the connector and a community cultivator and leader. As such, my new primary question shifted to: "How can I appreciate even more the connections, blessings, and success I already have?" Asking myself this new primary question motivated me to really tap into my connections and resources. To share more of those connections and resources with the people within my network and utilize my blessings to help others achieve their goals and success.

In addition to Date with Destiny, the other most impactful thing I invested in for myself has been Entrepreneurs Organization (EO) and, more specifically, my EO Forum, which has helped me achieve so many breakthroughs. One of the most insightful shares from one of my forum mates was the line, "suffering from self" because that is what many of us do when we dwell in anxiety, depression, fear, or imposter syndrome. What I have learned is that it is okay to experience and feel these but not to dwell in them. Another major breakthrough that I gained clarity on from a mix of Date with Destiny and EO is that the suffering from self stems from selfishness. When you focus on yourself, you suffer. When you focus on serving selflessly, the anxiety, depression, fear, and imposter syndrome all fall away. It is no longer about you but about others and how you can help them.

This realization is what inspired and motivated me to finally launch my podcasts and YouTube channel after fear and imposter syndrome held me back from taking action for so many years. When I shifted the focus from me to how and who can I help? What is the impact I could make for that woman who I was 5, 10, 15 years ago? How many lives can I change? What about those children of immigrants? What about the Asians in America who don't see leaders like me publicly because we are suffering from self-doubt? How can I serve as a beacon of light to light the way for others?

In closing, if you are seeking clarity, experience shares, guidance, growth, or just support on your journey, please connect with and follow me on Instagram and YouTube. I would love to hear from you and create content to support your success journey! @catheykuo on both platforms but DM me on Instagram if you have specific questions or requests for content! Or, if you are a 7-figure founder or top real estate agent or investor, I would love to interview you on one of my podcasts, so please reach out, and we can get that scheduled!

About the Author

Catherine "Cathey" Kuo is an 8-figure real estate investor and a serial entrepreneur who has founded a 7-figure business as well as multiple 6-figure businesses. During her journey, she learned many valuable lessons through failures and became a big believer in failing forward and sharing how she overcame those challenges to help others. Cathey is a child of first-generation immigrants from Taiwan and has overcome many personal and professional challenges to achieve what she has today. Although she learned many lessons the hard way through experience and failures, she still credits a lot of her success to the amazing guides and mentors she's had the privilege of learning from throughout her life. Today, Cathey is a living example of the American

Dream. Her purpose now, in what she considers her 2nd phase of her life, is to light the way for others by utilizing the connections, experiences, and resources from her unique journey.

Cathey is a big believer that you can have your cake and eat it too; she is now financially free, purpose driven, and happily married. She has been with her husband Robert for 7 years and today they are thriving together; both personally and professionally. However, their lives and relationship have not always been smooth-sailing. Like any other successful endeavor, there were many challenges to overcome along the journey; they were able to 'grow' through and not just 'go' through the challenges together. As such, she is excited to share her story of achieving balance and holistic success in both life and love to illuminate the path for others.

Cathey's current business endeavors include serving as the Broker and a License Partner for Engel & Volkers Las Vegas, Asset Manager for an 8-figure commercial real estate investment portfolio, YouTuber, Podcast Host for two podcasts: RealRichWomen & Unfiltered Conversations with Cathey, as well as selectively assisting her legacy Commercial Real Estate clients and personal friends with their real estate transactions. In addition, Cathey is a member of the Forbes Business Council, serves as the Strategic Alliance Partnership Chair for Entrepreneurs Organization Las Vegas, the Founder of her non-profit organization "Female Founders Foundation", and an Amazon best-selling author of the book "Lead Like a Woman: Audacity".

Connect with Cathey

Email: Cathey@elitecre.us

Instagram: @catheykuo

YouTube: https://youtube.com/@CatheyKuo

LinkedIn: https://www.linkedin.com/in/catheykuo

CHAPTER 9

Amplifying Ingenuity with Tenacity

By Jennifer O'Neal

The worst someone will ever tell you is "no."
When that happens, say "thank you" and move on.
–Tom Ramos, "McDonald's Restaurant Franchisee (Retired)
and Jennifer's first employer and mentor.

How Tenacity Gave Them One More Day Together

EVENTS EXIST TO GATHER PEOPLE and tell them a story. Some stories commemorate milestones, envisioning futures at events like graduations and weddings. Others focus on the present, guiding us toward self-improvement. Some stories act as rallying points, uniting supporters for common goals and showcasing the potential of collective action. And some stories are about the past; celebrations of love and heartbreak for those who now only live in our memories.

Regardless of the story they tell, planning and executing events successfully is multifaceted, and those responsible for them often find themselves in vulnerable positions. In addition to whatever emotions they are feeling, they are coordinating services, locations, and technologies that may be unfamiliar. This is where we come in: to support people with audio-visual services that amplify the stories they want others to see and hear.

In 1999, my husband, Dave, and I co-founded Live Oak Audio Visual in Seattle, Washington, to provide services and support to amplify our client's events. Our events range from a simple sound system for a backyard wedding reception to large video and sound productions for major fundraising events and multi-day conferences. If we do our job well, our services are discrete yet critical.

In our twenty-five years of owning this company, we have learned that events also create another level of storytelling: the story of the event itself. Tales of obstacles overcome, successes and failures, lessons learned, and guest behavior all become part of the event's secondary story.

My Favorite Event Story: A Culmination of Sweet Sorrow

Over the years, we've witnessed and participated in thousands of event stories. But, when someone asks me, what event was the most impactful, what event tells you that you've made the right decisions, what event tells you it was all worthwhile, this is the story I tell. It's a story about a grandfather and his granddaughter.

We work with several different departments at the University of Washington, and in the spring of 2022, we were contacted by their Human Centered Design & Engineering department to live stream their June graduation ceremony. Their department boasts a high percentage of international students, and with COVID travel restrictions still in place in several countries, the event coordinators sought to incorporate live streaming to ensure that families could participate in this important day alongside their students.

After several weeks of planning, our team arrived ready to set the event only to find out that the entire UW venue team was sick with COVID and there was no one to let us in the room. Our client and the university performed heroic measures to find replacement staff to unlock the venue. At 9:15 a.m., the doors were finally unlocked and we broke speed records for setting up a multi-camera live stream with picture-in-picture ASL interpreters and live camera feeds to the venue. We started streaming at 9:50 a.m. with only 10 minutes to spare, and the live stream was flawless. For context, this would typically be a 2-hour setup. We did it in about 30 minutes.

At this point, the event's story was about different teams working together to overcome adversity, single-minded focus to get the job done, and giving graduates and their families the celebration they deserved. You could practically see Sylvester Stallone shaking his fists in triumph with the theme song from Rocky playing in the background.

But that wasn't the end of the story.

About a week later, I got an email from the event planner, again thanking us for a successful event. She also wanted to pass along a message she received from one of her graduates:

"My mom told me that my grandpa watched the graduation live stream this morning, and he was talking about how proud he was of me. I am a ball of emotions and really grateful for the work that is put into making that ceremony something he could watch."

Her grandpa passed away later that same evening.

The story of this event ended not with the imagery of an iconic boxer celebrating at the top of the stairs but with the sweet sorrow of two people being able to spend one last day together.

After reading this message, I sat at my desk and wept. It's not often I feel the deep impact of our work so poignantly.

But this story didn't start with the graduation. To know how a grandfather was able to watch his granddaughter graduate, we need to go back to March 2020, when I was at my breaking point.

Navigating Survival Through Small Wins

Those of us in the live event industry will forever be traumatized by March 2020. In the span of a week, we watched our businesses vaporize as live events literally became illegal. We all looked helplessly at each other as our livelihoods disintegrated. At first, I was paralyzed; nothing in our previous 21 years of business prepared me for the possibility of our business ending this way. There was rage, gut-wrenching sobs, and desperation.

The problem of salvaging our business seemed insurmountable. In the darkness of this moment, I remembered a technique taught to me by some pediatric therapy colleagues who work with children with developmental delays and disabilities:

If you don't see success with a task or activity, it means that the task is too big. Break it down into a smaller component. Still not having success? Break it down again. Keep breaking it down until you experience success, and that's your starting point; that's where you start building.

Saving our entire business was too large of a task to wrap my head around, and the very thought of it caused decision paralysis. We would not achieve success by trying to solve the entire thing at once. By breaking it down into smaller parts, we realized that it came down to only two questions:

- What do we need today (monetarily) to keep the lights on?

- What assets do we have that might be of value to other companies?

Once we were able to articulate this, it became clear that we could use our now-idle cargo vans as a fleet for other companies who were forced to adopt a delivery model for their goods and services but didn't have a logistics team in place. We picked up the phone and started making calls.

While Dave was busy reaching out to food companies, I started reaching out to companies that were shifting their manufacturing or services and would need a team to run local delivery routes. I also put these requests to my Entrepreneur's Organization network, and a chapter member was able to connect me to a food tour company that was shifting to meal boxes but didn't have a delivery fleet. It was an idea that had legs, and we were able to partner with two different meal companies using this model. Finally, a small win!

Now that we had some business, I needed people to drive the routes for us, as most of our regular employees opted to go on standby. One of our new partners had connections with the commercial drivers of a recently closed city touring company. As 1099 contractors, the drivers were not yet eligible for unemployment in the State of Washington and were extremely excited about the work. I got commercially licensed, enthusiastic people to drive our company vans through Seattle and surrounding cities. The guerrilla marketing aspect of having our logos visible in all the neighborhoods was a bonus! Another small success, so we kept going.

How Do We Save Our Business?

Even though there was a plan in place to solve the need for emergency revenue, I knew that this wasn't a long-term solution. Eventually, established delivery companies would catch up with demand, companies would go back to their previous models, or they would build their own delivery fleets. I returned to the question of how to rebuild our audio-visual company.

In the weeks after launching the delivery service, several things happened at once:

- It became clear that the original 6-week ban on live events and social gatherings was going to last much, much longer.

- Our nonprofit clients, many of whom generate at least 50% of their operating budgets through their annual fundraisers, were not going to be able to host these critical events.

- 3,000 sq ft of space next to our main office became available.

- Westside School, our son's former middle school, reached out to us about the idea of live streaming a virtual auction from their theater.

At the beginning of April, I made three decisions that were either going to help our company survive or put the final nail in the coffin. Throwing caution to the wind, I committed to the following things:

1. I was going to teach myself to live stream events. Up until this point, we had only worked with live events.

2. I was going to double our rent by signing the least for the 3,000 sq ft space next to us and build a live stream studio.

3. I was going to hire a female marketing team to help us find clients who wanted to try virtual fundraisers. As most event planners are females, I wanted a marketing team that organically understood the viewpoints, hopes, and fears of our clients.

And since we were blazing new trails, I would later add a fourth decision:

4. I was going to publish everything we learned to help other AV and event companies with this model.

This last decision was unique as our industry tended to be siloed up to that point. If we, as both a company and an industry, were going to survive, we needed to share what we learned and forge new collaborations. I felt it was important to adopt the "rising tide lifts all boats" philosophy.

Decisions were made, and my journey had only just begun.

The Leap Into Live Streaming: Learning The Skills

After saying yes to Westside School's virtual fundraiser, my timeline to becoming proficient in live streaming was less than 30 days. While I had used this type of software before, it was typically for passion projects such as streaming my son's roller derby bouts. To gain the skills I would need, both for this specific event and for the next two years, I did the following:

- I read every article on the Wirecast website, the live stream encoding software I was using.

- I read guides and watched videos by industry leaders such as StreamGeeks, practicing what I learned and hopping into as many forums as I could.

- I learned the technical signal flow of how to get digital content from my computer to streaming platforms such as YouTube, Twitch, Vimeo, and Facebook.

- I learned industry terms such as "lower thirds," "stream keys," "eye gaze," "constant bitrates," and "stacked shots" and how they relate to live stream productions.

- I learned how to cue stage talent in and out from pre-recorded media so they were prepared when the camera went live.

- I learned how to read and create technical run-of-show scripts with separate cues for audio, video, shot layouts, transitions, countdown timers, and media sources, later teaching other clients how to write them.

- When a client would ask if we could do a new feature or technique in a show, I would go into the studio and practice what they wanted until I had the setup and flow correct.

- I set up separate rehearsals with the client, walking through the entire live stream and solving any media or production issues.

- I learned to ask for help from people with this expertise.

- I learned to pay it forward.

The Test Run

I needed a small win before leaping into our first live stream with Westside School.

One of our staff members at the time, Glenn Cannon, is an extremely gifted musician, and he agreed to do a test live stream so I could practice my skills before the school fundraiser. We set up a small stage in the corner of our warehouse and streamed Glenn performing an acoustic version of his music to his Facebook page, which got over 10,000 views!

The First Live Stream: Westside School

The virtual auction was hosted on Friday, May 15, 2020, and we put it together in less than one month. Thankfully, we were partnered with Fred Northup Jr., a fellow Westside parent and talented auctioneer with a background in television production who generously offered his expertise. Our nerves ran high but having a collaborative partner makes magic happen. And the results were amazing.

Westside School was able to raise more money with the virtual auction than the in-person event the previous year. By raising over $240,000, and by lowering their expenses, they increased their net revenue by $80,000. In addition, it actually increased attendance and access to the event than in years past.

"Since the event was a success, it has started a conversation about how to do this again? With the cost savings and the decreased time commitment, it made us think: Could we do a combination of in-person and virtual (event) next year?" said Shoshannah Hoffman, Westside School's Community Development Officer.

This was the win we needed!

Setting up the Studio on a Shoestring Budget

During this same period, I booked the first two events that would be streamed from our studio (remember that 3,000 sq ft space I leased), which meant there was now a hard and fast timeline to get the studio set up. In addition to taking on something I had never done before, the following COVID, operational, and financial challenges had to be considered:

- Each element of the studio that a person might inhabit had to be a minimum of 6 feet away from the next element, vastly increasing the physical footprint of the studio.

- Audio visual equipment manufacturers and resellers were closed or doing minimal operations.

- Shipping and transportation services were shut down or severely delayed.

- We had not received any PPP or EIDL funding at this time, so this was being financed through delivery revenue and some small savings.

- We had never done anything like this before.

With these additional challenges, we had to get creative. Here are some of the ways we got scrappy to create the studio space:

- Equipment from our live event and hotel inventory and furniture from our main office were repurposed for the studio.

- Craigslist ads were scoured for offices that were closing and giving away their furniture.

- I found tall, black velour curtains on Amazon and repurposed them for stage drape.

- I ordered a green screen to hang behind the stage so I could create virtual backgrounds for clients.

- I collected all kinds of fabrics to hang as backdrops.

- I went to estate sales on "50% off" days and bargained for decor objects and fake plants to create different looks on stage.

- Long plumbing pipes were used as curtain rods across sections of our studio to create green rooms and client areas and to block off cold air and noise. We would later leverage plumbing pipes to hang lighting and other infrastructure.

- Dave and Glenn found heavy-duty 4' x 8' coffee pallets on Craigslist, creating stage sections and a wood backdrop from the materials.

- We asked our event friends with production and theater backgrounds to help us configure the equipment placement so it was comfortable to use.

- I had my Gen Z son teach me how to use Discord as a free communication tool so I could talk to the crew and clients during live streams since each station was so far apart.

At the end of May 2020, we successfully live streamed virtual fundraisers for Gatewood Elementary and Global Visionaries. While the stakes for us were high, they were even higher for Global Visionaries who had to raise $25,000 or be forced to close their doors. They were able to raise $30,000 through the live stream that night!

Over the next 24 months, I was able to grow our studio and put together mobile streaming systems so we could host events from client locations. Both our live streaming acumen and this new division of our company resulted in many new client relationships and unique events including:

- Live streaming from the surgery clinic of a cat spay and neuter clinic and including a "Kitten Cam" where donors were treated to a live feed of adorable, adoptable kittens during the fundraiser.

- Live streaming several of United Way of King County's "How to Cook the Perfect Steak with Ethan Stowell" events, a brilliant donor engagement idea.

- Hosting KISW's "Live Day" where we rotated many musicians through our studio and sent the live feeds to the radio station.

- Setting up a mini recording studio to help Seattle Cancer Care record, edit, and publish presentations from 55 world-class medical professionals for their annual board review conference, an event we continue to support today.

- Providing a COVID-compliant studio so that Northwest Wine Night could film several seasons of their show in a way that kept their host, staff, panelists, and guests as safe as possible.

The Importance of Staying Visible

One of the most critical aspects to me during this time was the idea of staying visible to our potential clients and the community as a whole. Being an event company, people would automatically assume that we were closed. I began by having our delivery drivers take scenic photos of Seattle while they were running their routes. I formatted them for Zoom backgrounds and made them available for download on our Facebook page.

My first hire during COVID was to bring on the talented marketing skills of Mikaela Bolling and Emily Trickey, co-owners of Brilliant Marketing. During our first meeting, we established the ostentatious goal of "making us look busy." My philosophy was that if we didn't look busy, people wouldn't hire us. One of the ways we did this was by publishing our knowledge about events and what we were learning, something I had never done before. This strategy is still in place today, and the approach has been so successful that it has led to us producing a first-in-our-industry guide for women presenters, the *Feminist Guide to Presenting*.

Find Your Cheerleading Squad

Through all of this, the biggest lesson I learned was how important it is to have someone, or a team of someones, who believe in you as a person. Toward the end of 2022, I was having a bad day and lamenting to my son, Zachary, that I would never be able to navigate the business through COVID. It felt like an impossible task, and I thought it was eventually going to beat me down. He stood in the middle of the living room and loudly told me:

"Look, *Madre* (he never calls me mom), COVID killed social gatherings, and you *literally* have a business based on social gatherings. Instead of giving up, you looked COVID in the face and made it your bitch."

While his statement wasn't 100% accurate, it was exactly what I needed to hear at that moment.

So, who are the people in your life who believe in you entirely? Who unabashedly roots for you even when things are dark? Is it your mom, who maybe doesn't completely understand the business but believes you can do it anyway? Is it your favorite cousin who is always ready to lend a hand or pick you up and take you shopping at Ikea? Find those people and hold on tight.

The Definition of Success

As I'm, hopefully, looking at our business from the other side of COVID, there are many ways I could measure our success. First,

I could simply say that we survived. That, in itself, is more than what happened to many of our event peers. Or I could say that our new live stream service offering helped our business grow to over 2x the size it was before COVID. I could also talk about all the new, amazing client relationships or the wonderful new staff we've been able to hire.

All of these would be incredible measures of success. But to me, the definition of success is the ability to give a granddaughter one more day with her grandfather. That's what makes it all worthwhile.

About the Author

Jennifer O'Neal holds a Bachelor's degree in International Relations & Trade and a Masters degree in Business Administration. She brings over 25 years of industry experience to her role as CEO, co-owner and co-founder of Live Oak Audio Visual. With a background in business management, marketing, and nonprofit fundraising and a deep-rooted passion for driving social change through powerful experiences, she has dedicated years to bringing ideas and stories to life.

Jennifer's passion lies in leveraging events as a platform for driving social change and amplifying community voices. Through Live Oak AV, she works tirelessly to ensure that every event, whether virtual or in-person, leaves a lasting impact. From collaborating with schools and nonprofits to supporting businesses and event planners, Jennifer's expertise ensures that each occasion is seamlessly executed and memorable.

Beyond her work with Live Oak AV, Jennifer is deeply committed to entrepreneurship and innovation. As the co-chair of Seattle's Entrepreneur Organization Accelerator program, she supports other business owners who are actively trying to scale up their companies. Jennifer believes in the importance of constant evolution and innovation, viewing entrepreneurship as a vehicle for addressing contemporary challenges and driving positive change.

In her free time, Jennifer enjoys hanging out with her husband, family, and dogs, traveling with her son, playing the ukulele loudly but badly, going to Brandi Carlile concerts, and finding antique treasures at estate sales.

Connect with Jennifer

Email: jennifer@liveoakav.com

LinkedIn: https://www.linkedin.com/in/jroneal/

Facebook: facebook.com/LiveOakAV/

Instagram: @liveoakav

Download your free copy of the "Feminists Guide to Presenting: AV Tips for Presentation Tips for Women, by Women" by visiting: www.liveoakav.com/blog/

CHAPTER 10

Unstoppable: How Tenacity Became the Driving Force of My Life

By Paola Carranco

WHEN THE OPPORTUNITY TO WRITE this chapter appeared, I immediately experienced, as many women do, impostor syndrome. Am I really a role model for tenacity? Is my story enough?

I started thinking of people who I think have amazing stories of tenacity:

- Thomas Edison's journey to invent the practical incandescent light bulb came to my mind. His approach to the thousands of failed experiments, encapsulated in his quote, "I have not failed. I've just found 10,000 ways that won't work," is a powerful lesson in perseverance.

- Then Carlos, a man I met some years ago, came to mind. He suffered an accident that caused him to suffer large burns on his skin and lose his sight. Not only has he managed to live a "normal" life, but he also provides for his family, competes in triathlons, owns two companies, is a speaker, and opens doors that many thought he never could.

- My thoughts continued to people more familiar: stories from my past and present from friends, my parents, and brothers. Even my kids and my husband started to inspire me with some "common and day-to-day" events that were so much filled with tenacity…

Tenacity isn't reserved for extraordinary individuals or monumental achievements but is a quality inherent in all of us.

In sharing my story, I hope to inspire readers to embrace their own inner strength, illustrating that tenacity is often displayed in everyday life. My story may not be one of widespread fame, impactful stories, or groundbreaking inventions, but it's a

narrative of resilience in a regular life filled with challenges...
such as many others.

In sharing my story, I hope to encourage you to believe in
your potential, maintain a positive attitude, stay flexible, never
stop learning, have a purposeful living, and inspire you to
recognize your own inner strength and embrace the tenacity
within you.

Overcoming Childhood Hearing Loss

At 10 years old, I was visiting my uncle, my aunt, and my little
cousins in Brownsville, Texas. I had saved for a long time to buy
a Walkman because I wanted to fill my days with music. I placed
a cassette in and, despite my excitement, I sensed something was
wrong. I couldn't hear some beats and parts of the song. The
notes seemed to fade into a hush in my right ear. I figured it
must be the Walkman's fault—after all, what else could it be?
But in a twist that would reshape my existence, I discovered that
the silence wasn't a technical glitch; it was a piece of me that had
slipped away.

I embarked on a medical odyssey, a young explorer
navigating the labyrinth of medical tests and white-coated

experts. The word "tumor" was whispered, a heavy word for my parents to hear and such small shoulders to bear.

Fear, confusion, and uncertainty became my uninvited companions. I watched as worry etched itself into my parents' faces. I was cocooned in their love and concern, but what haunted me was not my own fate—it was the pain I saw in their eyes.

The results came back: "We are not sure why; maybe it was the side effect of a medication you took or an illness, or maybe you were born with this, and you just noticed, but you have lost all hearing capability in your right ear and will never recover it."

With that news, a flicker of determination ignited. It was this unwavering resolve, this unyielding flame within me, that propelled me forward. I refused to act like a victim, to be sad and make others sad, and I refused to let my partial hearing loss become the defining trait of my existence. I refused to be confined by limitations. Instead, I sought to redefine the boundaries of my capabilities, to shatter the glass ceiling that threatened to stifle my potential.

Even with the right attitude, it's not all been easy. I have had challenges and bad experiences: a secret from a friend whispered in my ear that I missed, a conversation happening on my right side that I couldn't follow, a waiter waiting too long and feeling ignored, a medical test on one of my first job applications that I failed because of my hearing even when the job was going to be in a regular office. In that instance, I challenged the system. Why would someone be denied a regular office job when they had been in regular classrooms and office environments without performance issues? I got that dream job, and the company became my second home for more than 11 years.

The journey of overcoming my hearing loss has shaped my perspective on life. It has instilled within me an unwavering belief in the power of resilience and tenacity. I have learned that adversity is not a barrier but a catalyst for growth, an opportunity to rise above the limitations that society places upon us.

Triumphs in Open High School

The decision to enroll in an open high school system was not made lightly. It was a choice that required spontaneity and was influenced by a transformative experience abroad and a firm resolve not to let conventional schooling timelines dictate my academic progression.

At the age of 15, my family visited family friends in Minnesota. During summer vacation, I had the opportunity to extend my stay in the United States and immerse myself in a new educational culture. The prospect was both thrilling and daunting, as it meant living with strangers, navigating a foreign school system, making new friends, living without my family, and bridging language barriers. Despite the uncertainties, I chose to embrace the risk and embarked on a transformative journey that would shape my perspective on learning and life.

The stay there was challenging but a great experience. I became more independent, learned about different ways of living, and enjoyed a new life with new friends and my host family.

Upon returning to Mexico City, I was faced with the prospect of retaking the entire school year in my old school due to a system misalignment. This was not a path I was willing to take! Driven by pride and impatience, I sought alternatives that aligned with my ambitions and my eagerness to progress. The open high school system emerged as an unconventional solution, offering the freedom and flexibility I needed to advance at my own pace.

Joining the open high school system required careful consideration. Despite its lack of prestige and the diverse mix of students (many were rebels who were "invited" to leave the traditional education system), I recognized it as an opportunity to demonstrate self-motivation and discipline. It was a challenge to propel myself academically in a setting where structure was minimal, and success relied solely on my own drive.

I fostered friendships and engaged in experiences that brought joy and balance to my life. However, it was not without its challenges. The open high school environment presented distractions and a relaxed academic atmosphere, requiring extra effort to study. I persevered, pursuing an English teacher's degree, studying French, and gaining work experience, all while navigating the open high school system.

Balancing self-study with work commitments during high school was also difficult. It required meticulous time management, discipline, and a clear vision for the future. My mother helped shape my disciplined approach, ensuring that my schedule was well-organized and leaving little room for idle time. The discipline to adhere to this schedule was fueled by a desire to complete my high school education, be productive, and contribute to society.

One example that showcased my focus was when I faced the challenge of completing a year-long algebra course in just 2.5 months without a teacher or tutor. Without the guidance of a teacher, I relied on self-study. I dove into the material, meticulously analyzing problems, trying to figure out how a problem got to a solution, understanding the underlying concepts, and applying them on my own. All while my mind had many distractions: a boyfriend, other friends, music, and even my brothers making messes. But I was determined to ignore the distractions and force myself to focus. I still remember the sense of achievement I had when I passed that test.

Succeeding in the self-guided open high school system required self-motivation, discipline, and accountability. Navigating those challenges fostered adaptability and resilience. Achieving academic milestones, such as completing high school ahead of my peers, amplified my belief in myself and instilled a sense of confidence.

Corporate Tenacity and Leadership

In the corporate world, navigating diverse cultures within different companies presents a series of challenges that demand adaptability, cultural sensitivity, and strategic thinking. Each corporation has its own set of norms, values, and communication styles, requiring a high level of cultural awareness and the ability to adjust one's approach. Building trust across cultural boundaries and managing expectations are also challenges. Understanding how decisions are made and overcoming stereotypes and biases are crucial for effective intercultural interactions. Balancing global and local perspectives and cultivating resilience and flexibility are essential skills for success.

Through the experiences I have had in the different corporate companies and roles around the world in prestigious companies such as Unilever (the giant Anglo-Dutch FMCG), I learned valuable lessons about the transformative power of tenacity. Resilience in the face of adversity is key to navigating professional challenges.

The corporate world has shaped my approach to leadership, understanding politics and stakeholder management, emphasizing resilience, vision, adaptability, empowerment, learning from failure, and fostering a culture of innovation. These lessons have guided my professional growth and success. They have also provided insights that are universally applicable across various professional contexts.

The Founding of Talent Lab

As I ventured into the world of entrepreneurship, leaving behind the security of a corporate career, I was driven by a combination of personal aspirations, a desire for autonomy, and the pursuit of a more fulfilling professional impact. I longed to see my personal vision come to life. Entrepreneurship offered me the canvas to build something from the ground up, reflecting my values, ideas, and aspirations.

The decision to start Talent Lab was more than just starting a business; it was about bringing a personal dream to life. I envisioned a place where work resonated with one's values. One where individuals could shine as their authentic selves, could be successful in their different roles, and they could work for the important things, without politics or bureaucracy.

The early days were filled with excitement and trepidation. I made significant personal sacrifices, such as not drawing a salary for myself for almost two years, to commit fully to the dream I was building.

I began by leveraging my network; spreading the word about Talent Lab's unique value proposition. Every interaction was an opportunity to share our vision and attract clients. During those years, I spent countless hours outlining every detail and inventing formats, presentations, processes, and methodologies that would set us apart.

One of the most fulfilling aspects was forming a team that shared the vision and values of Talent Lab. We have and have had wonderful people in the team and have strived to create a space of high quality and performance, devoid of power wars or fears of betrayal. Talent Lab was meant to be an example in the industry and beyond.

Days in Talent Lab are a whirlwind of activity, challenges, and learning. There have been moments of self-doubt, but the belief in the dream, the deep impulse to overcome obstacles, and the support of my team always brought back focus. Seeing

Talent Lab grow from a mere concept in a PowerPoint to a thriving business that has given many families a means to live and enjoy what they value the most has been one of the most rewarding experiences of my life.

An example of successfully overcoming obstacles was Talent Lab's response to the COVID-19 pandemic. The team rallied together quickly to brainstorm innovative solutions to problems that were appearing. We developed solutions such as remote work enablement, leadership in crisis management, employee well-being and resilience programs, and open-learning programs such as our change management and agile certifications. These solutions didn't only save jobs and keep Talent Lab afloat during the economic downturn, they also helped enable our clients to adapt and experience better the big challenges of the pandemic, which was very rewarding for us emotionally.

Building a business from scratch in different countries further deepened my understanding of tenacity. It taught me that tenacity is not just about persistence but also about adaptability and finding solutions in diverse and challenging environments. Overcoming failures and setbacks reinforced the importance of resilience. Language and cultural barriers required persistence and a commitment to understanding and respecting different cultures. Building networks from the ground up demanded tenacity in networking, negotiating, and building partnerships. Resourcefulness and innovation have been necessary in the face of limited resources. And amidst all the challenges, maintaining the vision and purpose of the business was a testament to tenacity.

Talent Lab has been a journey of passion, resilience, and unwavering commitment to a dream. It highlighted the need for adaptability, continuous learning, and a strong team culture. It has deepened my understanding of tenacity as a multifaceted quality, encompassing resilience, adaptability, perseverance, and the continuous pursuit of growth.

Personal Strength in the Face of Loss

My dear father died of cancer in 2022. Navigating grief and finding a way to move forward can be a transformative experience. It reshapes our understanding of resilience and the driving force of tenacity.

Allowing time for emotions was crucial for me. I gave myself permission to grieve, cry, and be vulnerable. I understood that grief is a natural response to loss, and I needed to acknowledge and express these emotions in order to heal. Rushing the process was not an option; I needed to give myself the space and time to mourn.

I remember asking my father what he had left undone. He told me that he was writing a book with the important lessons he had learned during his life to help others. It had become hard for him to write so I spent many hours by his side, writing his memories and lessons. It was a time of deep connection, shared ambition, and growing admiration. He died before we could finish the book, and I promised I would see it to completion. While it has been very difficult, writing and reflection is my therapeutic outlet. It allowed me to feel close to my dad, keeping his memory alive in my heart and mind. And it has allowed me to be present as I am open to interpreting signs that feel like messages from him. It's been a wonderful way to honor my dad's memory.

Living out his values became the most profound way I found to move forward. I made a conscious effort to incorporate his teachings and principles into my daily life. Honoring his memory by embodying the way he lived life became a way to keep his legacy alive.

I committed to honor his life not just through memories but also by continuing to live fully. Embracing life's joys and challenges with the same strength and positivity he exemplified became my way of carrying my dad's spirit forward.

Loss may shape us, but it does not define us. We have the power to rise above and become unstoppable.

Tenacity as a Way of Life… Yes, Even When You Face Trauma

Tenacity is a force that combines resilience, passion, and unwavering commitment. Resilience acts as the foundation, providing the strength to endure hardships and overcome obstacles. Passion is the driving force, fueling persistence and giving purpose to the journey. Unwavering commitment is the anchor, keeping one grounded and focused on their goals and values.

Here's one example of embracing a challenge as an opportunity for growth: It was February 2021, Thursday at 8:00 pm. I gave my kids a goodnight kiss and went downstairs to have dinner with my husband. Fifteen minutes later, the kitchen door crashed open, and five masked men broke in shouting, holding my kids and pointing guns at their heads and ours. They tied us up, hit my husband with the gun, and started to steal everything they could. After an hour of mental and physical torture, they left. I thought it all ended there, but that burglary, that invasion, left us all with trauma, a scar of vulnerability on our family.

This traumatic yet pivotal event became the catalyst for a decision: to seek a change of scenery and a breath of fresh air by relocating to Texas and leaving the familiar and comfortable behind. Talent Lab and other business ventures found fertile ground, blossoming anew. We chose to interpret this not as an end but as a beginning for new opportunities and prosperity. It reinforced my belief in resilience and the ability to turn adversity into opportunity.

I believe that tenacity is not just about personal success; it is about setting an example that motivates and uplifts others. It is about showing that with determination and a positive mindset, any challenge can be overcome. By practicing tenacity as a way of life, we can inspire others to believe in their capabilities and approach life's challenges with courage and joy.

Lessons and Insights From Tenacity

In the face of life's challenges, there exists an indomitable strength within each of us that can propel us forward. This strength, this tenacity, is not just a personal trait but a beacon of inspiration that can ignite a chain reaction of positivity, resilience, and achievement. I have witnessed this transformative power firsthand, both in my own experiences and in the lives of those around me... Tenacity is everywhere!

One such example is my husband who has managed to stop smoking 3 packages a day to zero just by deciding it more than 18 years ago. Or with his business ventures, leading with unexpected turns and rising from the ashes many times, learning from experiences but not looking back!

Or my brother Beto. With the right motivation, he made the decision to change his life habits. He quit smoking, lost over 50 pounds, started exercising daily, and improved his diet. The change in him was astounding. He not only achieved his health goals but surpassed them. His example is a testament to the incredible impact that tenacity can have on our lives.

Another is my brother Luis, who built his business from scratch and opened two others in the midst of the pandemic experience. Instead of watching more Netflix, as many others around the world did, he chose to find new opportunities and provide opportunities for others.

And my kids who, after living through a very difficult experience with the robbery, managed to get out of their Post-trauma and rebuild themselves even better than they were before, showing it with many examples as they grow up! And well, my mother... the one who is the vivid example of tenacity (maybe this book should have her face in the portrait!)

Beyond my family are the many people with disabilities or conditions that I have had the privilege to know who defy what is possible and break their own limits. Their determination and joy in tackling these grueling courses are awe-inspiring. They are a vivid illustration of human potential and a powerful reminder that self-imposed limits are meant to be broken.

I invite you to reflect on your own tenacity. Maybe you will think the same as me... "I am not special or a real role model of tenacity!" Well, with all the examples I have given you... think twice, I am sure that you will find great examples in your own life.

Share your experiences, too. By doing so, I believe we will do more than just recount our victories; we will become living proof that challenges can be surmounted. This act of sharing and demonstrating tenacity serves multiple purposes:

1. It builds resilience in others. By showcasing our tenacity, we help others build resilience. It is a way of saying, "If I can do it, so can you." This message is particularly potent when it comes from real-life examples that people can relate to and draw strength from.

2. It spreads positivity and hope. Tenacity is contagious. When others see us facing challenges head-on and coming out stronger, it spreads hope and positivity. It reinforces the belief that with the right attitude and perseverance, one can navigate through tough times.

3. It is about the journey. Embracing joy as a way of life means facing challenges with a positive mindset and coping with setbacks by shifting the focus from what is going wrong to what is going right. These strategies have

helped me to sustain motivation, enhance creativity, impact team morale, improve my personal well-being, and build stronger relationships.

4. It encourages self-belief. Empowering others through our tenacity encourages them to believe in themselves. It is a way of demonstrating that with persistence, discipline, and courage, goals that seem unattainable can be achieved.

5. It creates a ripple effect. When one person is empowered, they, in turn, inspire and empower others. This creates a community of individuals who are more resilient, optimistic, and driven. Tenacity has the power to transform not just individual lives but entire communities.

6. By inspiring and empowering others through tenacity, we leave a lasting legacy. It is about imprinting the message that life's challenges are not roadblocks but stepping stones to greater heights. It is about lighting the path for others to follow and demonstrating that with tenacity, the journey of life, with all its ups and downs, can be a truly rewarding adventure.

Tenacity is a potent force that can shape our lives and the lives of those around us. It is a force that can propel us forward, even in the face of adversity. It is a force that can inspire and empower others to overcome their own challenges and achieve their goals.

As I reflect on the impact of tenacity in my own life, I am filled with a sense of awe and gratitude. I am grateful for the support and inspiration of my family and community, who have played an instrumental role in fostering my own tenacity. I am grateful for the opportunities for growth and development that continuous learning has provided me. And I am grateful for the challenges that have tested my resilience and fueled my determination.

Lastly, I can say that tenacity is not just a trait; it is a way of life. It is a mindset that allows us to embrace challenges as opportunities for growth. It is a force that can transform our lives and the lives of those around us.

So, let us embrace tenacity, let us share our stories, and let us inspire and empower others to become unstoppable!

About the Author

Paola Carranco is passionate about the power of people and their influence to evolve organizations.

She holds a BA in Human-Industrial Relations, a postgraduate in Change Management, and in Diversity, equity and inclusion from the University of South Florida. She is also a certified Life coach, a Scrum & Kanban Master, Agile Human Capital executive and is a faculty member at prestigious Universities.

With more than 20 years of experience in HR, she has lived and worked in different countries such as the USA, Mexico, Brazil and England.

In 2013, Paola founded TalentLab®, a company that serves more than 400 clients each year (such as Walmart, BBVA, Pfizer, Starbucks, DHL, Unilever, Kellogg's, Bayer, Toyota, Avon, L'Oréal, HEB, Nestle, etc.) with offices in the USA, Mexico, Colombia and Peru, from where they serve the globe by unleashing the potential of organizations through their people & their culture.

Paola has been recognized and honored by different organizations for her work in HR innovation, diversity and organizational culture change, leading her to be a board member and an esteemed independent advisor to high-profile companies.

She is a serial entrepreneur and investor, an active member EO (Entrepreneurs Organization) in Houston Texas, and has been part of its board in the Mexico city's chapter.

In addition, Paola is president of INcluye, a group of more than 75 organizations committed to Diversity and Inclusion issues, with the aim to create a movement that generates a mindset change, impacting thousands of people.

Connect with Paola

Email: paola.carranco@talentlab.group

Follow me on LinkedIn:

https://www.linkedin.com/in/paolacarranco/

CHAPTER 11

You Are Who You Think You Are, So Dream Bigger

By Gail Stouffer

I'M A FIGHTER, AKA TENACIOUS. Kind of a gutsy claim, right? Well, I've been tested over and over since I was a kid, and I keep coming back swinging. It's made me smarter, stronger, and more compassionate. It's also helped me understand that whatever today's situation might be, good or bad, it's a temporary condition. I've learned that fear during change is transient and is meant to be learned from and then used as fuel to fight and grow. I'm stubborn, it took a while to learn that. I wear my stumbles and traumas as badges of honor; battle scars, making me wiser, tougher, and worthy of my successes. I own two successful e-comm businesses with deep market penetration in the hobby kiln and industrial heat-treating industry. Breaking in was tough as it's male-dominated, and has been for my twenty-plus year tenure. I have a 25-year-old son and a previous 30+ year marriage. My current partner is a supportive, positive, and encouraging guy who enables me to strengthen my resolve and dig deep through the roughest times. Being an entrepreneur can be a rollercoaster, and having a partner that *gets it* is so important.

MY RESOLVE WAS TESTED EARLY...

I grew up struggling. My single, divorced, working mother had little education and no family support, raising two little girls. There wasn't much money. In 1970, she felt her only option was to find a new husband fast. She wasn't around a lot. She was raised in a time when women were dependent on men for their goodwill, and in our case, that goodwill included food, clothing, and shelter. My mother instilled in us, "Never be dependent on a man. Always have your own money." Those words sunk in, and I internalized them. My older sister, still a mentor to me in life and business, ended up doing much of the parenting. At fifteen, I dropped out of high school, without direction and on a nowhere path. My inner voice said, "You are better than this."

I got my GED (general equivalency degree) as fast as possible. I spent the next three years working as a dental assistant, just surviving. I was sixteen and looked twenty-five. It was a different time. Again, my inner voice told me, "You are more than this," so I applied to universities. I was told by every school that they don't admit people with a GED. Instead of accepting "no," I just went around the problem. I enrolled in community college. I spent a year there and worked full time and went to school fulltime. I paid for it all, no loans, and floated my own boat. Looking back, that took some guts. I moved on to junior college and did the entire thing again, with those "don't depend on anybody" words ringing in my ears. I was scared to death every day that someone might uncover my high school drop-out status, realize that they'd made a mistake, and then boot me out. But until then, I was going to fight my way through every door they'd allow me to open. I got good grades and developed a track record that allowed a four-year university to take a chance on me. I still had to work full-time while tackling school, but I did get to enjoy the full experience. I have to give some props to my mom for lending a hand when I needed books or some other school-related expense that seemed out of reach. I graduated college with a BFA in Public Relations & Communications.

Again, my inner voice said, "You are going to be a success," and I believed her...sort of.

BEWARE OF BEING TOO SAFE...

For a few years, I worked in corporate sales, marketing, advertising, and communications jobs, developing a respectable, successful, and very safe life and career. I married a college boyfriend, worked hard, had a kid, a suburban upscale home, a European sedan, etc. By all conventional measures, I was successful. I did what the inner voice said I could do. I was independent, but the fear of not really being good enough and being found out that maybe I didn't really belong there because of some childhood trauma (HELLO IMPOSTER SYNDROME) was always lurking in the background. I navigated through pretty successfully until 9/11/2001. The market plunged, and the corporate world came to a screeching halt. Depending on the business you were in, either things were fine, or your career was toast. I was working for a start-up outside of Austin at a company partially owned by Enron (that's a whole other story), and things did not fare well. Within 90 days, a huge chunk of the workforce was laid off, and I was out of a job for the first time ever.

LOOK FOR THE OPPORTUNITIES...

I realized that replacing my fat paycheck in a depressed market after a national tragedy wasn't going to be an easy task. My spouse encouraged me to pursue a hobby while I looked for a job (Code for "You are driving me crazy"). I loved doing ceramics in school, but it wasn't practical with a toddler, so I landed on metalsmithing and glasswork. This was a good substitute, but I knew next to nothing about it. I found a local metalsmithing teacher, took classes, and immediately fell in love. This would unknowingly set my career path for the next 25 years.

FIND WHAT YOU LOVE AND FIERCELY PURSUE IT...

Never one to do anything halfway, I dove headlong into metals and glasswork, and before long, I was making so much jewelry and had so much equipment and tools, including multiple kilns, that I had to start selling my work. My hobby had now become a business. I was eight months into my unemployed phase, and I realized that I was employed, and I loved it! I just wasn't being paid as well, and I'd better do something about that quickly Now, this is the part in a movie where there would be some ominous music playing to warn you something is coming! The *not being paid as well* part would come back to haunt me shortly. In addition, there's a lesson to be learned here about the importance of being informed of your personal finances at every turn and not just assuming your partner's got it under control when they say they do. In the words of Ronald Reagan, "Trust, but verify."

CAPITALIZE ON WHAT'S WORKING...

In selling my work, I quickly realized that my customers were just as interested in how the work was made as they were in the work itself. Fifty percent of my customers would ask if I taught classes, sold the tools, or knew where they could take classes. In sales, you should be an evangelist for the product. Unknowingly, I was an evangelist for the process. As a communications professional, I had years of experience presenting information and coaching teams, so teaching adults seemed like a no-brainer. I began to teach metalsmithing and fused glass workshops in the local and then regional areas. My neighbor offered to assist me and later became a business partner. We opened a teaching studio, supply store, and a retail gallery all under one roof. It was a unique space nestled in an artist's enclave in a well-established shopping area. It was a risk, but eighteen months after being laid off from my job, I had embarked on a new venture, and I was ready for reinvention.

AFTER A GUT PUNCH, BE RESILIENT...

The exact day before we opened the new shop, a call came from Visa that my credit card had fifty thousand dollars of debt on it that hadn't been paid in months. My stomach was in knots. I called the other card companies, and they, too, had big balances. The entirety of the full debt was about one hundred and fifty thousand dollars. I was literally sick. Even after putting myself through four years of college, I had only incurred twelve thousand dollars of student debt, which I diligently paid off with pride. I'd always been a person of big dreams, but not having any exposure to serious wealth that seemed like a ton of money to me. I had no idea how we were ever going to pay that off or how we had incurred that amount to begin with. I was a working-class thinker. For someone who wanted to be financially independent, I had allowed my husband to take over handling all the family finances, and I paid no attention. That was a huge error in my judgment. My spouse, who had been raised comfortably, had figured that the market had taken such a bad downturn during 9/11 that it "made sense" to invest his pay in the market instead of paying our bills first. So, he paid all of our bills for the entire eighteen months with credit cards, thinking he'd make a score on the market and pay our bills later. But that risk took much longer to pay off than he'd bargained, and we were stuck with the debt now. Needless to say, this event caused significant stress. All good intentions aside, this was a huge error in judgment, and it was now up to me to get us out of it.

TENACITY NEEDS FUEL...

They say that adversity breeds ingenuity, and for me, it did. It woke me up like a bucket of ice water out of a deep sleep. I dug deep and worked hard. I traveled the country, taught classes, made product, looked for items to sell, recruited other artist-instructors, developed vendor partnerships (many I still have today), and figured out other ways to build the business. I was "the talent," and I had a solid business partner who handled all the finance, HR, and marketing, so I couldn't just hustle and pocket cash from the business to pay off the debt. It took four solid years of tap dancing, risk-taking, and a ton of fear, but I built the business, took home a respectable income, and pulled down enough to pay off the debt. Finally, the debt was gone, and the business was healthy, and I was exhausted.

JUST WHEN YOU THINK YOU HAVE A PLAN...

Then, a wrinkle appeared. I'm not a cry-in-my-soup kind of girl. Outlook is everything! Soon after the store opened and in the midst of the debt issue, my sweet boy, who is twenty-five now and healthy, began having issues. To provide him privacy and spare you the pity party details, at five, he was diagnosed with several genetic medical disorders. This created daily guilt, mixed with tiger-mother advocacy for my special needs child while juggling the full-time demands of a growing business. I carried the conflicts of my tenacity to be financially independent, never knowing what choices were right. I hoped I was setting an example.

I'm sharing this piece of my story because no tale of business challenge operates in a vacuum, especially for women. We juggle it all as female entrepreneurs; whatever our own personal baggage might be, the societal pressures and mother guilt of not being there enough or in the *right* way, the stress of not being *wifey* enough, caretaker enough for parents, or being perceived as serious or smart enough compared to men. All of the "enoughs" we have to be just to make it okay to be ourselves.

WORK IT UNTIL IT DOESN'T WORK...

Despite all the obstacles, I put my head down and worked. I looked for every opportunity to become a thought leader in my industry and took it. I had top influencers in the market tell me that I didn't go to the "right" school, I was too old, and I was running the "McDonalds" version of art. Put-downs to scare me off. Men in the industry called me a kiln whore. The more they said I couldn't, the more I was driven to prove I would. It became a revenge game. I even went back to school and got a Master of Art Education degree to back up my legitimacy with real-world credibility. The business hit a certain level of success regionally and then we hit a wall. I had gained a national reputation, but our revenues reflected only regional market penetration. It wasn't good enough for the kind of independence I needed. The business had to get bigger, and it wasn't going to happen with just a storefront. We had to PUSH! It was time to launch the e-comm business. I'll spare you the history of the internet. We knew success would be a combination of the right timing, having excellent vendor partners who wanted to see us succeed, and a clear focus on customer needs that were not being served in our market. In 2007, the e-comm business took off like wildfire, and in a matter of thirty-six months, our revenues eclipsed the storefront's. In 2010, we rebranded and spun it off into a separate corporation. A few years later, as the e-comm business continued to thrive, we decided to close the storefront, first the gallery, then the supplies, and then the studios were closed. I finally stopped teaching and traveling six years ago.

WHEN THE VISION STARTS TO CHANGE...

Someone has to compromise their vision (that's the fish), or someone has to leave (that's the cut bait.) If you've read this far, you know I do not cut bait, especially when I built the boat and the pole. In 2018, I decided to come off the road and stop being the teacher/evangelist/thought-leader face of our brand. To grow, the brand had to stand on its own. I was comfortable but not really happily married. After 30+ years, my husband and I fell prey to what happens with many: We traveled for work, tag team parented, and grew apart. That's the generic version. He's a good man, we remain friends, co-parent well, and I respect him immensely. My focus for myself and for the business was to grow, expand, and thrive on a broader stage. My business partner and I did not share the same vision for the business. She is a smart marketer and salesperson who didn't share my passion for our core product or market. As I wound down my traveling and teaching commitments, we struggled to define a new normal and get on the same page. We couldn't agree on direction, vision, goals, or even our working hours. The disagreements became petty. The situation was untenable and toxic. I saw opportunities for growth in the market and was willing to take the risks necessary to achieve them. She did not agree the opportunities existed and felt the risks were unnecessary. She wanted to sell the business, and I did not. After a particularly ugly argument, she made an off-the-cuff remark. Something like, if I didn't like "it" (whatever "it" was we were fighting about that day), I could just buy her out. I felt she was insinuating that I couldn't run the business without her (By now, you know that telling me that I can't do something typically results in the opposite result). My resolve and tenacity to save my business from being driven into the ground from a lack of direction, vision, or planning toward my goal was being threatened. After seventeen years of building, I was not about to let that happen. So, with the help of my mentor sister, a fantastic attorney, some savvy friends, and our vendor partners supporting me, I made it through what was a pretty horrible buyout negotiation and closing. Taking risks gets easier the more times you do it. I could never have been confident enough to take on the debt of a buyout on my own had I not experienced paying off the $150k of debt years earlier.

DOUBLE DOWN ON THE RESOLVE; EAT YOUR WHEATIES...

I can't remember who said that luck is found at the intersection of preparation and opportunity. In the midst of the buyout negotiations, a student of mine was job hunting. It was luck that he was the perfect fit to help execute on the vision I had for the company. I hired him in January, and we closed the buyout deal in mid-March as the US went into COVID lockdown. As the horrible death count flashed on TV, people were told to stay home. At home people were pursuing artistic hobbies to pass the time, including glass fusing, ceramics, knifemaking, and jewelry casting and enameling. These hobbies require kilns, and they were purchasing these from us. Businesses that were once dependent on commercial heat treaters to temper their metal tools and parts were now faced with waiting long periods of time to get their products back. Now, businesses were bringing the process in-house, and this required a kiln. They, too, were purchasing from us. We were completely overwhelmed by the tsunami of business that headed our way, but we muscled through, and our revenues quickly tripled by the end of COVID, including a spin-off of a new industrial e-comm site just last year. We are projecting to end 2024 with quadrupled revenues from the buyout numbers, with more than 70% of that buyout loan paid off.

FINAL THOUGHTS ON TENACITY...

It's been a road full of ups and downs getting to this place, but the focus and resolve have paid off, and my tenacity has been rewarded. Nothing worth having has come easily for me or without its lessons. The overall takeaways for me have been that risk and fear are twin sisters; not identical but part of the same family, and they come as a package. They seem to be my traveling partners on my road to success. I define TENACITY as taking the risks and facing the fears, pushing through toward success over and over again, not stopping, blinders on, until you meet the goal. Damn right, sisters, let's go! On to the next adventure...

About the Author

Gail Stouffer is the owner of KilnFrog.com and Heattreatnow.com, the primary online suppliers of kilns, ovens, and furnaces in the hobby craft and industrial heat-treating markets. Gail is the mother of an adult son, and lives in San Antonio, Texas with her partner, Eric. She began her entrepreneurial journey as a second act, after a round of 9/11 layoffs from her very last corporate marketing job. Fueled by her Bachelor of Fine Arts degree from Long Island University and a joy for creating, teaching, and a passion to help others find their artistic voice. Gail opened a retail supply store, gift gallery, and teaching studio, selling glass, metalsmithing, and jewelry supplies. For years it was her devotion and obsession. A lifelong learner, Gail conquered a Masters of Art Education degree from Texas Tech University, while flipping her little storefront into a national ecommerce business. In 2010 she launched KilnFrog.com the premier online destination for kilns and related items in North America. Twelve years later she launched Heattreatnow.com which thrives with industrial customers all over the world. Throughout her career she has done it all; glass fusing, pottery, metalsmithing, flamework, printmaking, and crayons. Gail has taught technique and design to artists all over the world. She is kiln crazy, in fact she's obsessed! When she's not working with her team on building the business, you can find Gail traveling or creating something with a kiln in her own studio.

Connect with Gail

Email: gail.kilnfrog@gmail.com

LinkedIn: https://www.linkedin.com/in/gail-stouffer

Instagram: @gailstouffer

Web: https://kilnfrog.com, https://heattreatnow.com

CHAPTER 12

Our Struggles
Do Not Define Us

By Suzanne Doyle-Ingram

"YOU CAN'T TELL ANYONE."

Those words echoed in my mind as I sat in the neurologist's office, my world crumbling around me. At 19 years old, I had my whole life ahead of me. But with a diagnosis of epilepsy, everything changed in an instant.

I handed over my driver's license and car keys, feeling a sense of disbelief and anger. "I can't have epilepsy!" I exclaimed. "I have a job, I have friends! I am normal!" But the doctor was adamant. He was convinced that the fainting spells I had been experiencing were caused by temporal lobe epilepsy, and my life would never be the same.

At first, everything was terrible. I rode my bike in the rain, feeling the pitying stares of those around me. The medication they put me on made me feel awful, and with each visit to the doctor, they increased the dose. I insisted that I had never had a seizure, but no one would believe me. They treated me like I was handicapped, telling me I couldn't go to college because it would be too stressful.

I remember the feeling of despair that washed over me as I left the doctor's office that day. I felt like my dreams had been shattered, my future stolen from me. I cried for days, struggling to come to terms with this new reality. The medication made me feel like a zombie, robbing me of my energy and zest for life. I felt isolated and alone, unable to connect with my friends who seemed to be moving on with their lives while mine had come to a standstill.

What were my friends going to think? Would I ever be able to have a boyfriend? Or would people be afraid of me?

As the weeks passed, something inside me began to shift. I refused to accept this fate. I realized that I had a choice: I could either succumb to this diagnosis and let it define me, or I could fight back and prove everyone wrong. And so, with a fire burning in my heart, I made a decision. I applied to the University of Victoria to study Linguistics, and despite the concerns of my family, I moved to Vancouver Island, determined to prove them all wrong.

Life at school was a revelation. I thrived in the academic environment, soaking up knowledge like a sponge. I loved my courses and the intellectual stimulation they provided. The epilepsy medication still made me feel tired, but I refused to let it hold me back. I pushed through the fatigue, staying up late to study and pouring my heart into every assignment. I made new friends who accepted me for who I was, epilepsy and all. For the first time since my diagnosis, I felt like I was living life on my own terms.

It was during this time that I stumbled upon a notice for a group looking for literacy volunteers. I was shocked to learn that there were people in my community who struggled with reading and writing. Growing up, I had taken my own literacy for granted, never realizing that there were those who had been denied the same opportunities. I felt a deep sense of injustice and a burning desire to make a difference.

I attended the information meeting, ready to sign up, but some of the questions on the application form rubbed me the wrong way. They asked if volunteers would be willing to work with people with alcohol or drug dependencies, or with homeless individuals. I found these questions discriminatory and walked out, deciding to start my own non-profit literacy organization.

At 22 years old, with no money and no experience, I was determined to make a difference. I poured my heart and soul into this new venture, working tirelessly to bring my vision to life. I made posters, held information sessions, and recruited 85 university students as volunteer tutors. We raised funds, secured office space, and received donated computers. I contacted Frontier College, Canada's oldest literacy organization, and they flew across the country to help train our volunteers.

As I told the volunteer tutors, "First we teach someone that they can learn to read. Then we teach them how to read."

Our first program was at The Open Door, a drop-in center for homeless people and those living an alternative lifestyle. I called the program The Open Book. I knew I couldn't just march in there and offer help without understanding their needs. It took six weeks of consistently showing up before anyone approached me for assistance. Slowly, I was accepted, and people began asking for help with filling out forms, computer literacy, and other tasks.

I'll never forget the day I arrived to find a somber atmosphere at The Open Door. A homeless friend of theirs had passed away, and they asked me to help write a eulogy. As we sat together in that small office, reminiscing about their friend and sharing stories, I felt the true impact of the work we were doing. These were real people, with real lives and real struggles. They had been cast aside by society, treated as invisible and unworthy. But through our literacy program, we were giving them a voice, a chance to be heard and understood.

The Open Book was just one of six programs we established. We had programs at a high school for at-risk students, on a First Nations reserve, at a children's center, and even at William Head Prison. The idea of entering a prison terrified me, but I refused to let fear hold me back. I met with prison officials, passionately advocating for the transformative power of education. To my surprise, they were receptive, recognizing the value of providing inmates with the tools to improve their literacy skills.

I'll never forget my first visit to William Head Prison. As I stepped out of the golf cart, my heart was pounding. The idea of being surrounded by inmates was daunting, but I reminded myself of why I was there: to bring the gift of literacy to those who needed it most. I took a deep breath and followed my guide to the meeting room.

As I sat down with the inmates, I was struck by their eagerness to learn. These were men who had made mistakes, who had been labeled as criminals and outcasts. But in that moment, they were simply students, hungry for knowledge and a chance at a better life. They worked their tutors, reading stories, writing essays, and discussing the power of words. I watched as their confidence grew, as they discovered new talents and passions. It was a reminder that everyone, no matter their past or circumstances, deserves to be given a chance.

Throughout this journey, I learned valuable lessons about perseverance, compassion, and the resilience of the human spirit. I faced numerous challenges, from skepticism and bureaucratic hurdles to my own self-doubts. There were days when I wanted to give up, when the obstacles seemed insurmountable. But I remained tenacious, driven by the belief that everyone deserves the opportunity to learn and grow.

I remember one student, a young man named Allan, who had struggled with reading his entire life. He had been told he was stupid, that he would never amount to anything. But through our program, he discovered a love for books and a talent for writing. He wrote a story about his childhood, about the abuse he had suffered and the dreams he had for the future. When he read it to me, I cried. It was a moment of triumph, a testament to the power of education to transform lives.

Years later, I look back on this experience with a sense of pride and gratitude. The literacy organization I started continued to thrive long after I moved on, impacting countless lives in the community. It taught me that tenacity isn't just about overcoming personal obstacles; it's about advocating for others and making a difference in the world, one person at a time.

As I continued to navigate life with epilepsy, a nagging feeling persisted in the back of my mind. Despite the doctors' insistence, I couldn't shake the belief that I had been misdiagnosed. I had never experienced a seizure, and the medication seemed to be doing more harm than good. I decided to take control of my health and seek a second opinion.

After extensive research, I finally found a general practitioner who was willing to listen to my concerns. Dr. Watson was a compassionate and open-minded physician who took the time to review my medical history and conduct a thorough examination. To my surprise, she agreed that my symptoms did not align with a typical epilepsy diagnosis. She suggested that we start the process of gradually tapering off my medication, closely monitoring my progress along the way.

It was a slow and cautious process, but with Dr. Watson's guidance and support, I successfully weaned off the epilepsy medication. I never experienced a single seizure. It had been a misdiagnosis all along, a fact that was confirmed by further tests and evaluations. The sense of relief and vindication I felt was indescribable. I had spent years living under the shadow of a condition I never truly had, letting it dictate my life choices and limiting my potential.

Looking back, I realize that my journey with epilepsy, as challenging as it was, had taught me invaluable lessons. It had instilled in me a fierce determination to advocate for myself and others, to question authority when necessary, and to never give up on my instincts. Now, 30 years later, I am proud to say that I have remained seizure-free, a testament to the power of perseverance and self-belief.

This experience reinforced my belief in the importance of self-advocacy and the value of seeking multiple perspectives. It taught me to trust my own body and intuition, even when faced with expert opinions that contradicted my own experiences. It also highlighted the critical role that compassionate and attentive healthcare providers can play in a patient's journey towards health and well-being.

I think back to that day in the neurologist's office, when I was told I couldn't tell anyone about having epilepsy. I think about the fear and shame I felt, the sense that my life was over before it had even begun. But through my journey with literacy,

I learned that our struggles do not define us. We are so much more than our diagnoses, our labels, our past mistakes. We are individuals with hopes and dreams and the potential to change the world.

So, to anyone facing seemingly insurmountable challenges, I say this: believe in yourself, stay true to your convictions, and never give up. With tenacity and determination, you can overcome any obstacle and achieve the impossible. You have the power to rewrite your story, to create a future that is brighter than your past. And along the way, you might just change a few lives, including your own.

About the Author

Suzanne Doyle-Ingram is the founder of Prominence Publishing and the creator of The Expert Author Program and Book Publishing Made Simple.

She is a best-selling author who has written and co-written over 20 books, including her most recent best seller, *Everybody Has a Book Except You.*

Suzanne coaches and trains business professionals on how to write, publish and leverage a book to promote their brand and business. Her programs and services help authors increase visibility, secure speaking opportunities, attract new clients and grow revenue.

With a BA in Linguistics, Suzanne brings a love of communication to her writing and publishing initiatives. She speaks English, French, Japanese and recently traveled for 3 months in South America to learn Spanish.

Since 2010, Suzanne and her team have helped over 1,000 business professionals write and publish books.

Connect with Suzanne:

Prominence Publishing: https://prominencepublishing.com

Free training: https://prominencepublishing.com/free

Facebook: https://www.facebook.com/suzannedoyleingram

Instagram: https://www.instagram.com/suzannedoyleingram

LinkedIn: https://www.linkedin.com/in/suzannedoyleingram

Have you always wanted to write a book? Apply for a Discovery Call with Suzanne and learn how easy it can be to finally get your book out to the world:

https://prominence-strategy.youcanbook.me

CHAPTER 13

Latin Tenacity

By Krisana Puccio

THOUGH BORN AND RAISED in the United States, my heart beats to a Latino rhythm. My father comes from Costa Rica, but Spanish was not spoken in our household growing up. Traveling each year as a family to his home country, I was drawn to the rich, vibrant culture, always wanting more after each visit. In fact, at 17, I had the opportunity to spend a semester in Costa Rica attending high school. Inspired by this unforgettable experience, I arranged to work as an intern in Costa Rica for a summer during college. After graduating from college with a business degree into a challenging job market following 9/11, I dedicated three life-changing months volunteering in Oaxaca, Mexico.

Largely because of these fulfilling experiences in Latin America, three years later, I chose to pursue an MBA at INCAE Business School, a highly regarded institution in Costa Rica. Of the 90 students in our class, 89 were born and raised in different Latin American countries. I was the oddball from the United States, and though I did speak conversational Spanish, I was not prepared to learn in Spanish at a business school level in a fast-paced program that was structured to test the limits of students' resilience, analytical skills, and ability to manage stress.

The first 16 weeks felt like an endurance test. As the only non-native Spanish speaker, I had to work twice as hard as most. I would hear or read the material in Spanish, then internally translate it into English for comprehension. After processing the information, I would translate my thoughts back into Spanish before expressing them. This continuous mental exercise of decoding and recoding was not only time-consuming but also mentally exhausting. Moreover, my ability to participate in class—a heavily weighted component of our grades—was limited.

All MBA students were required to live on campus during the two-year program. Unmarried students lived together in four-bedroom houses, with two students per room. My housemates were from Costa Rica, Guatemala, Honduras, Panama, and Venezuela. Understanding some of them felt impossible. I knew that accents, vocabulary, rate of speech, and grammar varied among the different Hispanic countries, but I had not expected such drastic variations. My roomies and classmates were patient and understanding, but I felt alone and out of place.

INCAE used the case study method, so I spent countless hours in the library each day, working through pages of complex, jargon-filled Spanish text. The reading felt like an endless endeavor, and when finished, I attempted to solve the cases. Students were encouraged to gather in groups to discuss and resolve the case studies, but since my reading pace was much slower, my classmates were often well into the group work by the time I was able to join them.

Between the translating, the case studies, the fast-talkers, and other social pressures, I felt completely depleted at the end of each day. Sleep did not come easily, as it was hard to quiet my overworked brain. However, I was determined to stay the course. A classmate from Peru helped me tremendously. Excelling in finance and accounting—areas that were particularly challenging for me—he was patient and held faith in my ability to succeed. Eventually, as my Spanish improved *poco a poco*, I began to thrive in the program both academically and socially.

As I evolved into a proficient bilingual business school student, my interest in the language and culture of Latin America grew even stronger. The nuances of Spanish from different countries were fascinating to me, and I loved the challenge of incorporating the vocabulary and slang from each country into my own Spanish. I strangely enjoyed that outsiders struggled to pinpoint my origins.

Fast forward five years, and my husband (the patient, Peruvian *amigo* mentioned above) and I were living in San Antonio, Texas, both enmeshed in fulfilling yet demanding jobs at a fast-growing IT hosting company. As we steadily grew in our corporate careers, he and I shared a dream to run our own enterprise someday. Each weekend, we indulged in a ritual—brainstorming business ideas over breakfast at our favorite Tex-Mex restaurant. On one particular Saturday morning over a plate of *chilaquiles*, the idea came to me: a high-quality child care center that offers Spanish and cultural immersion; a safe and dynamic place where children learn a second language as they are learning their first.

In the weeks that followed, I mulled over the concept. What a perfect opportunity for young children to be exposed to a second language during a period in which their brains are like sponges and primed for language development. How else can a monolingual parent (in the United States) feasibly help his/her child to acquire a second language? The opportunities I had in Costa Rica and Mexico were invaluable to me, but for most parents without family ties in Latin America, securing a study abroad experience for a child can be overwhelming, risky, and very costly.

I drafted a business plan that demonstrated strong ROI. The key success factor would be to operate with strong enrollment. To achieve and maintain strong enrollment numbers, I resolved to deliver a high-quality, knock-your-socks-off level of service for young professional "working" families in San Antonio.

My mother, with training and experience in early childhood education, was recruited to join our venture. In order to secure the multi-million-dollar SBA loan needed to purchase property, build a facility, and cover operating expenses, my husband and I depleted our savings. This was not enough to cover our portion of the down payment, so we borrowed additional money from a family member. As excited as we were about the project, the debt we were swimming in was massive.

During the development stages of our project, my mother, husband, and I continued working our full-time jobs. This left us nights and weekends to select and purchase property, work with architects and builders, research and develop the curriculum, write policies and procedures, purchase equipment and supplies, draft and carry out a marketing plan, hire and train staff, recruit families, and make ongoing important decisions about the program. The process was grueling, and the stakes were high.

At the time, language immersion programs were just beginning to come about in large metropolitan cities like San Francisco, Boston, and NYC. But the concept had barely made its way to San Antonio, or really, Texas, for that matter. This posed a significant challenge because, in addition to convincing parents to entrust us with the care of their most prized possessions in a brand new program, we had to educate them on

Spanish Immersion—what it is, what the benefits are, and how it works within an early childhood curriculum.

I distinctly remember a parent who came to the school for a scheduled tour and immediately noticed a sign that read *"Bienvenidos,"* the word for "welcome" in Spanish. He asked why the sign was in Spanish, and as I started to explain that this was a school where children would be immersed in the Spanish language and culture from the moment they arrived, he turned around and walked out the door, commenting, "Why would I want my kid to learn Spanish? We speak English in the United States." This was not the only encounter with this type of reaction, but I continued to push forward. I researched the benefits of bilingualism and multilingualism. I posted articles on our social media that supported our cause and developed talking points to address the concerns.

We opened The Pineapple School on a summer morning, welcoming, on day one, 50 students ranging in age from 3 months to 5 years. While I was happy with this number as a starting point, I knew it was insufficient for sustaining operations. Our commitment to providing exceptional care for the children and building trust with the parents would be crucial for boosting our enrollment numbers.

Over the next several months, we faced unanticipated challenges. The school was burglarized twice within a two-month period; the intruders gained entry by breaking windows. We discovered that a key staff member was being dishonest, which resulted in her termination. Our head *cocinera* (cook) walked out one morning, never to return, and many of our recipes went missing. Due to a broken pipe, two classrooms flooded on "Parent's Night." We terminated services for a child due to extreme behavior challenges, something we had not anticipated having to do. A nasty but acute virus called Hand, Foot, and Mouth Disease, causing mouth sores and a rash on the hands and feet, swept through a classroom. Though quite common among children under two, I had never heard of this illness and was humiliated that it had made its way into our school. By mistake, there was a time I did not click the submit button to process payroll, and staff members, rightly so, were very upset. Because it was the first of the month and rent was drafted from their accounts automatically, some suffered overdraft charges.

Because the school was newly established, these obstacles were intensified. We did not have protocols in place or prior experience in the industry to guide us. Additionally, I was sleep-deprived and overwhelmed. With two children under the age of two, nights were tough, and even during their moments of rest, I often found myself caught in a cycle of overthinking and rumination. However, amidst these challenges and the distractions they created, we remained persistent and steadfast to our mission, learning from our mistakes and upholding transparency to preserve the trust placed in us by clients, employees, and investors.

In spite of these obstacles, the journey was profoundly gratifying. Our students were thriving in the program. Thanks to the patience and determination of our amazing team of teachers and staff, children were engaged with bright eyes and high energy, and they were embracing the language and culture of Latin America. Pleased with their child's experience, parents began to enthusiastically recommend our school to friends and colleagues.

Within one year, the school was at capacity, with 155 students enrolled. We implemented a waiting list and were blown away when it developed into an average wait time of two years. The school earned a strong reputation in the community and was able to depend on word-of-mouth referrals, almost exclusively, to maintain enrollment. Running the business was becoming more manageable. I was able to start collecting a salary, albeit feeble, and to take a day off from time to time. My own children were thriving in the program and were speaking fluent Spanish. Having the opportunity to bring them to work with me was an invaluable blessing.

Five years into our journey, we expanded by opening a second, somewhat larger campus eight miles up the road. Armed with the experience gained from the first project, the process was considerably smoother and more manageable. *¡Menos mal!*

It was five years later, during the construction of our third and even larger campus, that we once again encountered challenging circumstances. March 30th, 2020, was set to be a big day for us, the grand opening of our newest school. When COVID-19 hit San Antonio on March 13th, everything changed, and we were forced to delay.

Two months into deliberating the opening of our newly constructed campus, we ultimately chose to embrace the risk and proceed to open our doors. We had a beautiful 16,000 sqft. building (and a hefty mortgage to go along with it), a newly recruited team of employees that needed work, and at least a handful of families that were in dire need of childcare. The circumstances were far from ideal, but the alternative of not opening was grim.

Meanwhile, we continued to run our two existing schools without closing a single day throughout the pandemic. Because both schools served families of doctors, nurses, and other essential workers who needed reliable care for their children, we kept our doors open, following recommended modifications to provide a safe place for children and staff.

The next year was gut-wrenching for me as the owner of three childcare centers. While I felt grateful for the opportunity to help families during these uncertain times, it was an overwhelming responsibility to protect the well-being of our children, our staff, and their families. The livelihood of my own family was also a significant concern.

There was no playbook for navigating COVID cases among childcare centers. The information that was available to us changed from week to week. Like the rest of the country, our Pineapple community was deeply polarized on issues such as masking requirements, isolation periods, vaccinations, and the confidentiality of those infected. The decisions that we made in response to the ever-changing landscape, which were always based on research and opinions of experts, seemed to split parental opinions down the middle—half in support, half in outrage. The prospect of sending COVID-related updates to parents filled me with apprehension. My stomach would churn each time I pressed send, as each communication would inevitably result in a deluge of email responses ranging from strong support to almost forceful opposition.

Moreover, I had serious concerns about our financial situation. With attendance dwindling and many families withdrawing their children, I was not sure how long we could go on. At the same time, I was committed to providing continued employment for our staff members. My anxiety was higher than ever before. I cried daily. I tossed and turned at night. I persisted, and we eventually made it out of the woods.

Today, our three schools proudly employ 150 Latina women and two very brave men. They serve approximately 575 children and boast an average Net Promoter Score of 9.6, as rated by parents. At The Pineapple School, children are happy, engaged, and inspired to learn and grow. *Maestras* are warm, affectionate, and energetic. Our nurturing yet vibrant atmosphere is captivating for the children and their families alike. Motivated by our desire to impact more lives, our next venture is to franchise The Pineapple School. This expansion will allow us to extend our unique educational approach to more communities, more families, and more children.

I will candidly confess to anyone who asks that I am not someone who possesses remarkable intelligence or creativity; I am not a business guru, a leadership expert, or a visionary by any stretch. My success hinges on a quality that I believe is inherently present in all of us—tenacity.

To be tenacious is to embody a keep-on-trucking (persistent), roll-with-the-punches (adaptive), stick-to-your-guns (adhere), and bounce-back (recover) mindset. By acknowledging and nurturing this powerful inner strength—tenacity—dreams are transformed into *realidad*. As I embark on new ventures with my family, a single quality will propel me through inevitable adversity and toward my goals: my tenacious spirit.

About the Author

Passionate about education, language, entrepreneurship, and all things Latino, Krisana Puccio dreamt up the idea of a Spanish and culture immersion child care center circa 2007. Today, she is a proud co-owner of The Pineapple School, with three campuses serving nearly 600 young children in San Antonio, Texas. In a bold move to expand the impact of her vision, Krisana has partnered with her sister to grow The Pineapple School through franchising. Before embarking on this entrepreneurial journey, Krisana honed her skills in product marketing, digital marketing, and public relations while working at Rackspace Technology. She earned an MBA from INCAE Business School in Costa Rica in 2006 and a Bachelor of Business Administration from the University of Texas at Austin in 2002. Krisana serves as a volunteer mentor for young adults who have aged out of the foster care system with an organization called THRU Project. As an active member of the Entrepreneurs' Organization (EO), she continuously seeks opportunities for transformational growth, both personally and for her business. In her free time, Krisana, a self-proclaimed health nut, enjoys playing sports and exercising, caring for her 40+ houseplants, reading, and traveling. She and her husband, from Peru, have been married for 18 years; they have three amazing children who are growing up far too fast and two zesty dogs.

Connect with Krisana

Email: krisana@pineappleschool.com

Facebook: https://www.facebook.com/krisana.puccio

Instagram: @krisanapuccio

Instagram: @thepineappleschool

CHAPTER 14

The Unexpected Journey
From a Small Town
to a Global Life

By Sarah Endline

MY MOM ALWAYS USED TO tell me as a little girl, "Cool your jets." I guess I didn't really listen.

Today, I'm a serial impact entrepreneur and an Executive Fellow and Entrepreneur in Residence at Harvard Business School and the Harvard Innovation Lab. I am advising the next generation of entrepreneurs and incubating Sazzy, another new global venture of my own.

My entrepreneurship began early on but was in one tiny place. I grew up in the Tri-Cities—an area of Michigan including Bay City, Saginaw, and Midland. However, I was in Auburn, the small farm town sandwiched in between these three cities.

My grandparents were farmers, and my parents were small business owners. I was very rooted in the same town for my entire childhood, growing up in my great-grandfather's large, old-fashioned, and airy white farmhouse surrounded by large stretches of beautiful open corn fields. My favorite places in our home were my shared room with my older sister with unicorn and rainbow wall paper on the walls or the old chicken coop my parents had turned into a playroom. Indeed the chicken coop was a place of fantasy and play, and there were Barbies and Smurfs inside.

I created my first candy company in elementary school and was CEO of my Junior Achievement companies in high school, specializing in wood crafts and personalized playing cards. During high school, I was also busy as Class President at Bay City Western in Auburn and in the arts in the neighboring towns of Midland or Bay City.

I grew up in a town of 2,000, but my grandparents and parents had a surprisingly global mindset. I was curious about living abroad. It began with looking at month-long programs, and suddenly, I was applying for a year-long scholarship. I knew there was a world out there but didn't know it fully. My life was changed when I was selected for CBYX in Germany.

With Congress-funded schooling and an internship in Cologne and Bremen, I discovered AIESEC and went on to be the National President in the USA. I spent the summer of after my program traveling through Dresden, Leipzig, Krakow, Budapest, and Prague as the new Eastern Europe opened.

The global life was beginning.

After university and AIESEC, I was an early Internet pioneer and began working with digital initiatives at NFTE.com fostering entrepreneurship education online in NYC. Before, during and after grad school, I was engaged early on at Yahoo! and Microsoft's msn.com. I was designing and launching products and marketing programs for millions of consumers during the internet's infancy in the late 1990s.

I came back to NYC from San Francisco and Silicon Valley with a dream of my own company.

As a long-time social entrepreneur, I am motivated by the change I can create in the world. Simon Sinek, the best-selling author of Start with WHY, personally helped me develop my WHY—To build a sweet movement to fix the world!

When I started sweetriot, I dreamed of disrupting an industry. I thought of Ben and Jerry's and their crazy ice cream story and Anita Roddick, the founder of the Body Shop, which disrupted cosmetics to be socially responsible. Coming from Yahoo, I wanted to create a product I could put in people's hands. The Internet was never something I could carry around or take as a house gift. This connection to physical products likely also related to my farming background. The land is so tangible. The harvest creates physical products.

I was not a chocolatier or a crazy chocolate lover, but I started selling M&Ms at the age of seven, so I thought to myself, why not disrupt the candy industry?

The problem was I knew nothing about candy, chocolate, factories, or retail. Unless you count my elementary days of candy sales, of course! I needed to teach myself and fast. As one of my mentors, Steve Mariotti, used to say, "Make yourself an expert!"

I started going to every food and candy show I could find—Expo West for organics, NCA sweets and snacks for candy, and Fancy Food for gourmet products.

I was unsure of where to focus and what product category to build on. On a whim, I decided to move to Hong Kong for the summer. I loved Hong Kong and China from prior work there and luckily had some college friends all based there at that moment. Someone offered a couch, and I was off! I figured there must be a diamond in the rough I can find in Asia.

I bought a one-way ticket and landed on my first couch, Adam's, in Hong Kong.

As I was thinking of changing the candy industry, I thought first of lollipops and gummy bars. Luckily, there was a lot of production of these products in China just outside of Hong Kong. I had a list of names from the candy show and slowly set up appointments all summer long to visit each factory.

I remember traveling to Shenzhen and visiting my first ever factory in China. I could see the swirling barrels of multi-colors before the gummy bears were set.

I marveled at the remote location of so many of these factories in the middle of what seemed like the countryside.

Not long after landing in Hong Kong, I started to wonder if these sugary products were *the future*. I would go every day to the Foreign Correspondents Club (FCC), my home away from home, and read and research the industry. I started to think that perhaps chocolate was the bellwether of the candy industry and the true center of it.

I would ride the escalators up and down the Mid Levels of Central Hong Kong and wondered if I was going in the right direction with candy. I started to wander into the Life Café on the escalator. Life Café was a favorite natural food shop and had a clean and spiritual vibe. Up at the top of the escalators was the Hong Kong Natural Coop Store. I would wander the Coop aisles looking at products. It seemed to be that many of these products there were "the future of candy."

My first focus group was held in Adam's high-rise building. I can remember the all-glass view of the gorgeous Hong Kong skyline and the boot-strapped focus group I was holding. Every person I knew in Hong Kong was invited, and I had prepared a paper plate tasting with a survey to follow.

On the paper plates, I had numbered products I had found in either China or in the health food store in Hong Kong. I wanted to hear from this group of young professionals which products they liked and wanted to purchase. Needless to say, the healthy products won by a landslide. This may all sound obvious, but remember, this was 2004 before the dominant healthy food movement began.

I realized it was time to go back home to NYC to change my product direction. The interesting natural products I found in Hong Kong weren't even Chinese; they were American! Luna Bar from CLIF in Berkeley, Ospri from Wisconsin, and more. I knew the diamond in the rough I sought might just be something like healthy dark chocolate.

This newly energized focus on chocolate was as important as my research proved; the largest sales across the candy industry were dominated by chocolate. Chocolate was the bellwether of the industry. In my view, if I wanted to change the whole industry, I needed to start with the core and center point of the industry, which was chocolate. As I dug further, I realized the true center was the cacao fruit!

Through sweetriot, I am proud to have launched the world's first line of healthy chocolate cacao nibs and to be an early and award-winning innovator as a fair trade, organic, and B Corps certified company.

sweetriot sold millions of units and impacted thousands of Latin farmer's lives and profiled numerous emerging artists. Over several years, I worked closely with my board to drive the company to an exit to a cacao company that would carry on this mission.

Luckily, during this exit, I was asked to be an Entrepreneur in Residence at Harvard Business School and am actually the first social entrepreneur ever to receive that honor.

As part of my global life, I guess it's not surprising that I married a French man. That was natural. Life honestly seemed perfect. An inspiring business and a romantic and global life.

It was the divorce that was most disruptive

Divorce is never easy, but imagine sitting home alone during a global pandemic, considering your choices. By April 2020, I was clear. I was in New York City (NYC). He was in France. This was not a marriage. Despite every call to him, I felt unsupported and alone.

July 5, 2020, is a day I will never forget. It was our six-year wedding anniversary and 12 years together. He answered the phone, and I said, for our anniversary gift, I'm going to set you free. You are miserable, and this is the best gift I can give you. He tried to argue that it was COVID, but the marriage was already over, and my decision was not negotiable.

In the summer of 2020, the best advice a friend gave me was that, despite the fact that the paperwork wasn't finished, I needed to start living my life as a newly single woman. This wasn't meant to be about dating or freedom as much as it was about reshaping my life.

I did not realize then that the hardest part about divorce (for me) was rethinking how life looks. I had spent the last 12 years in a 2 country life with a business in NYC, stepchildren in

France, and holidays most often across the Atlantic. We shared our main home in NYC but kept a small place in France. I was accustomed to working mobile, traveling easily, and being a part of the children's lives as a stepmom.

Suddenly, this all seemed to be unclear and crumbling. I wondered if I had to negotiate for a relationship with my stepdaughter. I wondered if France was going away.

I entered December of 2020 in a complete fog. I pondered if I should sit at home for New Year's Eve to avoid any social interactions during my sadness. Luckily, a dear Turkish friend invited me to sit outside in Miami, and it became a magical night near the water. Things started to become a little clearer. The New Year's Resolution 2020 into 2021 was then set... It was a choice. I needed to create a New Life. I just did not even imagine I could make my life global once again.

This was when the Tri-City life began, but this time, it wasn't a small part of Michigan. It was three cities across two continents. My new homes would be NYC, Miami, and Paris.

How, you may ask, did this occur? It was a simple choice. With today's technology and the internet, many forms of entrepreneurial work can be performed anywhere.

My stepdaughter was an anchor in France. My Michigan family was an anchor and are now in Florida. My long-time business friends and family were in NYC.

I divested a property in NYC and secured a storage unit. I researched ways to land in these three places in a more mobile way. I found the furnished apartment in Miami, the French-decorated homes in Paris, and the sublets in NYC.

It wasn't easy, but it began with a simple choice. I did not want to be in one place. I did not want to be a nomad. I wanted to be rooted again, like in small town Michigan, but this time rooted in three places.

We probably can't imagine what this choice would have been like in the 1920s—no planes and no internet. Today's world is different. The internet gives us unparalleled access to information, and airplanes give us access to new worlds, which brings me to a story about planes.

I learned about the 747 as a little girl. Although I grew up in a small town, my parents always looked out for the international incentives they could win by being strong small business insurance owners. My father won one and went on a trip to Japan; he came home with endless stories and gifts, including a kimono, which we found to be so exotic.

When I finally had a chance to ride a 747 as a grown adult, I was thrilled. The memories of that kimono came rushing back, and it was like I had suddenly arrived in the world as an adult being allowed on a large and beautiful airline.

One day in 2017, I learned the 747 would be making its final trip to Europe before retiring the planes in favor of those who "guzzled less gas."

I researched the information and learned there was a flight from San Francisco to Frankfurt, and it was during the dates I normally traveled to France for my stepchildren's school vacation. Perfect, I thought! However, I also realized I was based in NYC and would be in Atlanta the day of the flight, speaking to students at the annual Net Impact conference. I am never willing to cancel something I committed to, so I had to find a way to San Francisco for this flight via Atlanta.

I knew it was not ideal to book an indirect flight from Atlanta to San Francisco/SFO, but I wanted to stay on United due to my status and their flexibility.

As I left the conference that morning, I rode with a group of students in a "mentorship" Lyft, and it was a fun and inspiring ride full of chatter about their futures. I paid for the Lyft to the airport and then sent them round-trip back to the Net Impact conference. My flight from Atlanta to Denver was on time and worked smoothly.

However, upon landing in Denver, I started to see a delay on my San Francisco/SFO flight. I asked United if perhaps San Jose/SJC was possible, and they moved me to this flight. After moving to this gate, I learned they were also delayed. Unfortunately, SJC is only 34 miles from SFO, but on a Friday afternoon in Silicon Valley, the highways are packed and full of bumper-to-bumper traffic. This could easily take 1.5 hours! I knew that things were starting to look very risky for my flight connection.

I sat down on the SJC flight in a newly acquired middle seat, and my seatmates could tell I was nervous and asked why. I told them about the 747. One instantly connected me to his driver in SJC, and we booked him for my arrival before I even left Denver. The other passenger just wished me luck for the "risky attempt."

Upon landing at SJC at 5.30 pm, Mohammed was waiting for me. I hopped in the vehicle and explained my need to reach the 7 pm 747 flight. He looked at me with wide eyes, as he knew this was quite a difficult request.

Mohammed was a great driver and weaved in and out of exits as best he could to make up time through the traffic. However, the reality was clear: I could not reach SFO until 6.42 pm for a 7:00 pm flight.

Thank goodness I thought of tweeting United about the dilemma. I was quite clear with United that I was trying to catch the final 747. I sent them photos of my special outfit with my 747 memorabilia attached.

United on Twitter instantly replied, asking about my flight numbers, my checked baggage, and my exact whereabouts. After a few exchanges, they gave me clear instructions to enter a domestic door upon arrival that led me directly to the domestic Global Services entrance. It seemed there was a chance I could make it!

Mohammed pulled up to SFO. I rushed through the Global Services door and had a person waiting at the end of the security belt. This small Asian woman, I wish I remembered her name, ran me over to an empty gate and down a jet bridge. At this point, I was confused but simply following her. She suddenly opened an outside door, and we were heading downstairs to a waiting United-branded Mercedes Benz on the tarmac. At least at that point, it felt like I was in the right place.

She and I went zooming across SFO to the international terminal, and she took me up a secret elevator to the indoor gate area. She pointed me toward my gate, and I ran. I'll never forget the photo of the clock at that gate—6.47 pm. I ran down the jet bridge and snuggled into my upper deck first-class seat. I was in a state of shock as the jet doors instantly closed, and the plane started rolling seconds later.

That evening on the plane, I really couldn't sleep. I was so excited the entire time. I stood to walk around the upper deck sometime in the middle of the night, and only the flight attendant and I were awake. She asked me if I had seen the aurora borealis, and I said, "No…" She led me to a window with the most magnificent view of the sparking Northern Lights. I couldn't believe my eyes!

Upon landing, the 747 was met with a firefighter salute. Fire trucks on either side were spraying water over the plane in an amazing archway. Crew members were standing on the tarmac waving as the plane rolled in. Upon exiting the plane, a large mural of the plane was on display, as well as a cake with a 747 on top, flowers, and 747 postcards. The pilot stopped to pause with tears in his eyes.

The moral of these stories is that crazy dreams are good! Don't give up on them too easily. I was seconds, minutes away from missing that flight! However, it was a choice to go for it.

It's a choice to be global. It's a choice to be an entrepreneur.

My mom always used to tell me as a little girl, "Cool your jets." It is true -- I didn't really listen.

About the Author

Sarah Endline is an Executive Fellow & Entrepreneur in Residence (EIR) at the Harvard Innovation Lab & Harvard Business School. Sarah is a serial founder especially focused on consumer innovation, impact, digital art & collectibles. Sarah was launching products at Yahoo! during Web 1 in Silicon Valley & uses the past to predict the future.

Sarah is now incubating Sazzy out of her post at Harvard. Sazzy is the Etsy of digital collectibles – a shopping emporium going after the $200 billion dollar plus self-expression market for women. Sarah's contrarian approach is to create the next wave of digital collectible adoption by building a shopping and collecting experience for women with NO trading in the design.

Sarah last built and sold sweetriot in NYC - a Certified B Corps, Fair Trade, Organic, & Inc. 500/5000 company. Sarah's creations have been covered by The Wall Street Journal, NY Times, Forbes, & Fortune. sweetriot was a Whole Foods partner for over 10 years.

Sarah is an entrepreneurship speaker for US Embassies worldwide and a scholarship funded Harvard MBA, Michigan BBA, public school graduate from a small farm town in Michigan.

Sarah builds sweet movements to fix the world and this is the next one!

Connect with Sarah

Email: sarah@sazzy.io

Phone: 1-917-304-2255

https://calendly.com/sarah_endline

NYC – Paris – Miami

CHAPTER 15

Rule Number One: Know Your Worth

By Sarah Dray

AS I SAT IN MY BOSS'S office, feeling the tears well up in my eyes, I thought to myself: "This might be your most embarrassing career moment yet."

Unfortunately for me (and him!), no amount of internal begging prevented those inevitable tears from spilling over. What followed was a kind of stunned silence while I pulled at my sleeves, and he shuffled through his drawers for a tissue.

"Listen, I'm sorry," he said. "We just can't afford to let you take those eight days of Passover off. I understand that you want to spend it with your family, but it's a busy time of year."

I mumbled something, left his office, was confronted by a secretary who was very surprised to realize that I was in tears, and shuffled back to my office—dejected.

Allow me to backtrack.

I had worked unbelievably hard to get the chance to begin my career at a big law firm in the heart of Tel Aviv. In fact, I had moved to Israel at 18, enrolled in law school in Hebrew (despite having shoddy Hebrew language skills at best), and climbed metaphorical mountains to find myself exactly where I was. And I wasn't happy.

I had zero control over my time, I wasn't earning enough to make a dent in my bills, and I was less than thrilled by the work I was doing. I remember being put on a case defending an insurer against a compensation claim by the family of a mine worker killed in an unfortunate work accident.

As a young intern, I didn't know much, but I knew that this wasn't doing it for me.

How It Began

What followed that conversation with my boss was one of the major crossroads of my life: the decision to continue to pursue the already long-traveled path to a career in law or to take a sharp left and start over.

Spoiler alert—I started over.

My life has involved a series of dramatic resets, some of which I initiated and some of which were serious blessings in disguise.

After having moved to Israel at 18, likely in search of stability and also as a result of being in an Ultra-Orthodox community, I decided to get engaged at 19 and married the following year.

During my seven years of marriage, I practiced Ultra-Orthodox Judaism, followed extremely strict dietary laws, wore only very modest clothing, and even covered my hair with a wig. It was extreme. All the while, I attended law school, began my internship, passed the Israeli bar exam, and started a translation business as a side hustle.

Trying to navigate law school in a foreign language was my first true head-on encounter with tenacity. Always a bookworm, I had excelled in school growing up and hadn't faced any significant challenges. On the contrary, I was used to being top of my class and was fortunate to have amazing parents who prioritized my education, even helping me skip from 5th grade straight to 7th grade in an effort to challenge me. I don't know why I assumed law school in a foreign language would be just as simple, but I did.

During my first semester of law school, I can honestly say I only understood about 40% of what was taught in class. This was before Wi-Fi was available in the classrooms, so I sat in the front row with a language dictionary and frantically looked up every other word. I would then create flashcards and test myself on the new words every night.

I'll never forget our first homework assignment: to summarize an article and present our position. The assignment was not allowed to exceed one typed page. I started it the night before it was due (old habits die hard) and ended up pulling an all-nighter, searching for each Hebrew letter on the keyboard one by one, trying to research the correct grammar, with my head stuck in a Hebrew-English dictionary. I got a 44.

With the help of some very special people, to whom I am eternally grateful, I was able to graduate law school with a GPA that I learned to love, and even set up a side-hustle as a freelance translator, which supplemented my student wages working on campus for the North American fundraising office.

Little did I know that this freelance translation work would evolve into something bigger and greater than I could have ever imagined, ultimately giving me the freedom to own my own time, put myself first, and take home more than the senior partners I started my career under.

The Epiphany

It would have been cinematic, perhaps even poetic, to say my moment of clarity came amidst a blaze of glory in a high-rise law firm, where I, in a defiant act of rebellion, ripped to shreds a 50-page M&A agreement and declared to my boss with unwavering conviction, "I'm out!! And I won't be coming back." But life, in its unscripted reality, chose a far less glamorous stage for my epiphany.

Instead, there I was, in my pajamas, hair a mess, the clock barely striking 5:30 AM.

Surrounded by silence, I realized no amount of coffee could chase away the deep-seated exhaustion. As I set to work on the translation project due by 9:00 am (sharp!), the absurdity of my situation struck me. I was looking down the barrel of a gun: finish the project, dress quickly, catch a bus to Tel Aviv, and spend a grueling 10-12 hours at the office. In that stark, predawn moment, the glamour I once associated with my career dissolved, unmasking an undeniable truth.

I wanted better.

I was dreaming of something that I didn't know was possible. I wanted to make a ton of money, but I wanted freedom. I wanted to work hard, but I wanted the right to choose how and when.

Having realized over my three years of freelance translating that there was a huge demand for high-quality translations in the legal field, I decided to go all-in.

Becoming My Own Boss

Before I knew it, my 12-hour days at the office were replaced with 12-hour days on the couch (my home office).

I began reaching out to every translation agency that I could find on Google, offering my Hebrew to English translation services.

It wasn't long before I had four big clients who kept me extremely busy.

I translated for as many hours of the day as I possibly could, with the help of my husband at the time, who supported me immensely and who would tag-team proofreading legal text with me.

A few years later, I had more work than I could handle, and I knew I wanted to expand my team.

Looking at the industry, I noticed that not many translation companies hired full-time translators. I struggled with the idea of training freelance translators and sharing my valuable knowledge with potential competition, so decided to take the plunge and hire attorneys who wanted to leave the industry and try something that offered them more flexibility.

It was a painful "what am I doing" moment when the overhead became too much to handle. Evidently, there was a reason why translation companies were not hiring full-time translators, and I had just discovered it. The hard way.

I knew that I had made a mistake, and I truly dreaded the idea of firing these excellent people.

Admitting a mistake is never easy, especially when it involves risking the livelihoods of those you've brought on board with a vision of change. The realization that I had veered off course was daunting, yet it underscored a critical lesson for me: flexibility is not just a bonus—it's a necessity.

I had to pivot, and fast. The decision to transition from a traditional full-time model to a more dynamic, project-based team structure was both a return to my roots and a leap into the unknown. I focused on building a network of freelance professionals, offering not just work but a collaborative partnership in which I trained them and shared my corrections to their work. This shift was extremely powerful—not only did it reduce overhead, but it also allowed for a broader range of expertise and flexibility, aligning more closely with my vision of freedom and autonomy.

The Power of Resilience

When I look back to the early days, I am surprised by how much resilience I demonstrated.

Around the same time as firing three full-time employees, my marriage collapsed. I was 27 and my friends were all getting married and starting to have kids, and I was ever-so-painfully going back to square one.

I remember being invited to a costume party and deciding that it was the perfect opportunity to dress up my adorable little pup as a Minion. My dog, now a four-legged beacon of despicable cuteness, was all set to be the life of the party.

As we strutted into the party, I quickly noticed the sea of little superheroes, princesses, and assorted fairy-tale characters. It dawned on me—everyone else had prepared adorable costumes for their human offspring, and I was the odd man out. There I was, standing in a room full of parents proudly showing off their kids, while I proudly showed off my...Minion-dog.

I realized in that moment that there was no room for me as a single woman in suburbia; I had to move out into the city.

Difficult days followed, but to me, resilience isn't about being tough, putting on a brave face, and stoically moving forward.

It's about confronting yourself—with everything that entails.

It's about crying into your pillow at night and waking up the next morning with the hopes of tackling the day.

It's about knowing that somehow you always end up right where you need to be and that your challenges are your biggest opportunities to level up.

So I showed up, started over, and put in the work.

Building the Business of My Dreams

Building the business of your dreams is absolutely possible—as long as you successfully discern what your dreams actually are.

For many years, while I was trying to grow my business, I didn't really ask myself what I wanted to gain from it, what I hoped it would look like, or how I anticipated my future in the business. Instead, I just built businesses the way I expected or imagined that businesses should be built.

It wasn't until I was confronted with this question by an incredible business coach that I started to pick apart my expectations and assumptions.

I discovered the following: 1) I assumed that making money necessarily involved hard work; 2) I assumed that training people to my standard of quality was not possible; 3) I had created a self-imposed ceiling of what financial success looked like.

Of course, like many of our beliefs and assumptions in life, they were the product of my upbringing and based on encounters I had experienced or my interpretation of certain influences. The truth was that they were all holding me back.

The business that I run today, and that serves as my primary source of income, does not require that I spend 10+ hours a day translating like I used to. It relies on the exceptional efforts of wonderful, hard-working people whom I trained, and—to my great surprise (and joy and relief!)—the financial rewards of running the business this way did not decline when I stopped doing all of the heavy lifting myself—on the contrary.

Questioning all of these assumptions has allowed me to create a business that aligns with my vision, values, and personal goals. I strongly encourage everyone to spend the time writing or talking with a friend or family member about what assumptions or expectations you have of success. At a minimum, it'll start the process of getting you into a success mindset, and at best, it will help you pinpoint your self-imposed limitations, and over time, you can release them and build something greater than you ever imagined.

The Elephant in the Room: Fear of Failure

Having a lot of easy successes early in life is fertile ground for deeply rooted fear of failure. This was one of the biggest personal challenges I had to work through early in my career and personal life.

Luckily for me (wink wink), I encountered so many ostensible failures that I was left with no choice but to overcome this fear, which had only ever held me back and kept me small.

Each stumble and fall, while initially bruising my ego, slowly chipped away at the colossal wall I had built around the possibility of failing. I began to see these not as stop signs but as detours, ones that often led to unexpected paths of creativity, love, and innovation.

Failure, I realized, wasn't the opposite of success—it was a critical part of it. The "failures" became lessons, some harsher than others, but each one invaluable. From the ashes of a failed engagement, I learned the art of never settling. From the collapse of a promising deal, I learned the virtue of patience. And from the disintegration of what I thought was a bulletproof plan, I learned the power of adaptability.

The fear of failure never completely dissipates; it's an intrinsic part of being an entrepreneur—and a human. But instead of allowing it to paralyze me, I now acknowledge its presence but never let it overstay its welcome. Embracing the fear of failure is akin to taming the elephant in the room—it's still there, but now it listens to me, not the other way around.

This newfound relationship with failure didn't just liberate me; it also became the bedrock upon which I built the business of my dreams. It allowed me to take calculated risks, invest in people and ideas, and create a company culture where "failure" isn't a dirty word but a stepping stone to greatness.

Dreaming Even Bigger

Five years after getting divorced and moving to the big city, I found myself (note the passive voice) engaged to someone who ticked every item off my checklist: British, doctor, kind, funny, smart, on the same page as myself religiously.

Imagine my surprise when, 34 days before the wedding, he woke up, looked at me, and said: "Sarah, I can't do this. I'm going to work now; when I get home, I'll pack my things and go."

The initial shock was mind-numbing. The calls to the wedding vendors were grueling. I remember sitting next to my mom when my uncle called after "hearing the news." Being the source of collective pity was truly my worst nightmare.

Four months later, I realized that I was still very much dealing with the aftershock and that I needed to get away.

Being an entrepreneur is wonderful, but I had found that there was no such thing as a real vacation when the business was always "my problem." This time, I decided, I really needed a break and would go to any length to get it and clear my head.

My team was amazing and supportive, and my 2-week trip to Thailand with my mom was made possible by their hard work and dedication.

While I was there, contemplating my relationship history and what could have possibly led to the end of my engagement, I decided to put pen to paper and write out what I could bring to a relationship and what I dreamed my future partner would be like.

And let me tell you—I dreamed big. I didn't hold back on imagining what my perfect partner would be like. I described how he would treat me, what values we would share, what personality traits were important to me, what quality of life I was looking for, and more. Engaging in this exercise proved to be not only therapeutic and revelatory but also, in the fullness of time, prophetic.

Fast-forward another four months, and I was sitting at a sushi restaurant with a new friend, going through the pros and cons of getting back together with my ex-fiancé, who had only recently apologized profusely and promised a future of marital bliss.

"Let me just give my cousin your number. He's been asking about you for a while after seeing pictures of us on Instagram," she said.

My jaw nearly dropped at the suggestion. I was currently dating someone, my ex-fiancé was begging for me back, and it really felt like my love life was complicated enough.

Despite my hesitation, she gave him my number, and we scheduled a date for the following night.

We both left that first date knowing that we would end up married—it was *that* good, and the connection was *that* instant. A few weeks later, while scrolling through my camera roll, I saw the screenshot of the perfect partner description that I had written and realized that I was currently dating him.

We moved in together four months later, got engaged eight months after meeting, and were married 10 months from the night of our first date.

What sounds like a fairy tale ending was preceded by countless struggles, hundreds of bad dates, thousands of dollars on therapy, and never giving up.

Reflecting on my journey, I marvel at the distance traveled. The road was anything but straight. It was a path filled with more twists than I would have wished for myself. Yet, each bend brought with it a new perspective, each setback a fresh challenge.

If I could have a chat with my younger self, the one who thought tears were a sign of weakness and a 44 on an assignment was a sure failure, I'd tell her this: "Sarah, you're going to take this world by storm. Those tears? They water the seeds of your growth. That 44? Your Hebrew will get so good that you'll be CEO of a leading translation business in the country. And every 'no,' every rejection, every stumble? They're just lessons that will drive you forward until you find exactly what it is you're looking for."

So, take it from me—someone who has fallen many times but got up one more time than she fell. Your path is yours to forge. Let the fear of failure be a chapter, not your story's title.

Don't wait for the stars to align; align your actions with your aspirations and set those stars in motion yourself.

Now, go out there and write your own success story—one courageous decision, one belly laugh, one tenacious comeback at a time.

About the Author

Meet Sarah Dray, a licensed attorney in Israel, CEO of Dray Translations, and the entrepreneur behind a 7-figure Amazon business. Bridging cultures through legal translations and dominating the digital marketplace, Sarah embodies tenacity, transforming challenges into opportunities. Her career showcases innovative business strategies and a commitment to leadership excellence.

In "Lead Like a Woman," Sarah shares insights from her multifaceted journey, offering a unique perspective on being a self-starter and never settling. Beyond her current business ventures, she dreams of launching a course to empower individuals to start successful side hustles, sharing her blueprint for creating multiple income streams.

Sarah's story is an inspiring blend of resilience, innovation, and unwavering ambition, encouraging readers to lead with tenacity and creativity. Her vision extends beyond breaking barriers, aiming to redefine success and inspire action.

Eager to learn more or collaborate? Sarah invites you to connect with her on LinkedIn. Join her network to explore opportunities, share ideas, and be part of a community striving for greatness. Search for Sarah Dray on LinkedIn and reach out—she's looking forward to connecting with fellow leaders and aspiring entrepreneurs.

Connect with Sarah

Email: sarah@draytranslations.com

LinkedIn: https://www.linkedin.com/in/sarah-dray/

Instagram: @drayster817

Looking forward to connecting!

CHAPTER 16

Lead Like a Woman

By Tracy Marlowe

I LOVE THE WORD TENACITY. Yet, I don't know that it is a word I would have used to describe myself prior to my collaboration in this book. As I reflect on my life though, and the journey I took to get where I am today, I realize that tenacious may be a rather precise description of the woman who took that journey.

And where am I today?

I am the CEO and owner of a creative branding and advertising agency that has developed and stewarded numerous brands, both small and large, in its twenty-plus years of business. Our primary focus, and one of my primary business passions, is helping our clients authentically inspire and connect with their audiences.

I am also a leader who has built a company upon the principle that if you invest in women, you will consistently see exponential returns within business and the communities in which they live.

I'm also a mother. While motherhood hardly defines me, I find I am learning every day that the best way to raise two happy human beings is to always choose love, first and foremost.

Last, but certainly not least, I am a woman on a voyage of self-discovery. I am leaning in and digging deep to do the soul-searching work and try to uncover my purpose all the while learning to embrace my imperfections. It turns out that the best path to fully loving those you care about is to love yourself first.

What has been tenacious about my path? We often wish our life journeys were whiled away on a well-paved, straight road without any hills or potholes. No rain, ice, or high winds. Just a sunny drive with the windows down on a scenic country road.

The universe has proven one thing to me over the past fifty-plus years. You never know what is around the next bend in the road, and it is most often that pothole-laden, unpaved road that will provide insights into your true character and teach you what you are truly capable of.

My path to where I am today was far from straight and easy. Some of the more rugged terrain in my journey has included starting a marketing business at the crux of the 2008 Great Recession with a new infant at home. Next came scaling my company while raising two children and navigating countless ups and downs, including accelerated menopause, a devastating divorce, and a global pandemic. I've learned that women are incredibly resourceful. When we believe in ourselves and our mission, we can accomplish pretty much anything we set our minds to.

Parenthood is perhaps one of life's most profound teachers. I was late to the role, not having my first child, a daughter, until the ripe old age of 36. A geriatric pregnancy, they called it. I had my son a week before my 39th birthday. Three years later my body threw in the towel, and I was fully post-menopausal. That in itself is a chapter for another book!

My husband initially didn't want to have children. He was divorced and was worried that having children would change our relationship. In my heart, I believed ours was a love for the storybooks. I finally convinced him that he was wrong and that our path would be different than it was in his first marriage. How naïve I was about the impact motherhood would have on me. And us. And my career.

One vasectomy reversal and five years of infertility treatments later, we had our daughter. She rocked my world. Her sweet, fierce, joyful spirit suddenly turned everything I thought I knew and wanted on its head. I was fully committed to climbing the corporate ladder at the time. As an incredibly driven advertising executive, I had found my superpower was digging deep down inside my clients' companies to unearth their true essence. I would then turn that research into incredibly authentic brand platforms from which we would build robust and powerful marketing programs. The success I was having for my clients was intoxicating and addictive. Yet this eight-pound human being suddenly shifted my center of gravity, becoming the sun in my universe.

There I was at the height of my young career, having led multimillion-dollar rebrands and campaigns with global giants. Yet suddenly, having a corner office or a Vice President job title and the salary to go along with it seemed far less imperative. Being the best mom I could became my core focus. As my success at work grew, so did my work hours. I found myself working late many nights and calling home to ask my husband to put our infant daughter to bed. I felt horribly guilty and knew I was missing precious time with her that I would never get back. It wasn't sustainable.

I finally decided to quit my job. I didn't have a plan. I just knew that I had to find another way to do work I could be proud of while not sacrificing motherhood. Six months later, I started my company, Creative Noggin. I had three core principles at the time: First, I would only work with nice people—nice clients and nice employees. The advertising industry is known for having an ego or two. To work with or for us, you needed to check your ego at the door. Life is far too short to work with prima donnas.

Second, I would only work with clients who believed in the work their company did. "In it for the money" was not a motivating enough factor. I find it is much easier to develop compelling marketing for a company when you know they are doing the best job they can for their own customers—whether it be a children's mental health hospital or a propane company. If they are excited about the work they are doing, that excitement is infectious and easy to get behind.

Third, I had been an employee and knew what it was like to work for somebody else. I wanted to create a company that was very employee-centered and where people felt valued. This tenet evolved into the mission of the company. The company was initially developed to empower me as a new mother, allowing me the balance to have a fulfilling career doing work I loved while still having critical time with my family.

When I started my company, I realized that most of my clients over the past five years had never set foot in the fancy conference rooms of the agencies for which I was working. When an in-person meeting was needed, I went to my clients' businesses. The internet had been a game changer and allowed for a paradigm shift from the usual agency model as most of our work was being conducted online. Many companies were also beginning to question their high monthly agency retainers and wondering what those fees were covering.

After a lot of reflection, I made the decision that we would operate fully remote. This was a pretty new concept pre-pandemic. We didn't hide the fact that we operated remotely. We were proud of our decision and how it differentiated us and we made our remote model a part of our company branding and marketing.

Instead of hiring a handful of senior level leadership to lead and win business with a stable of young talent to actually execute the work, we decided to flip that business model on its head. With a fully remote workforce, we could invest instead in all senior-level, experienced, and specialized talent. We would also not be limited by the confines of our local talent pool, allowing us to search far and wide to find the best talent who fit both our culture and modern marketing needs.

Our clients loved that the people pitching the business were the same people doing the work. They also found themselves paying more reasonable hourly rates for senior-level talent because they weren't also paying the overhead of a physical office

LEAD LIKE A WOMAN

location. It was a model that attracted smart clients who were seeking higher returns from their marketing spend. They loved the formula and referred us consistently to their colleagues. I never could have anticipated such growth, and we ended up growing an average of 296% yearly from 2008 to 2012.

I found over the years that this business model was increasingly attractive to women. Up until I started my business, I had worked in more traditional office settings. I saw that the traditional eight-to-five business model felt very designed around "a man's world." Most working women in the U.S. are also responsible for a disproportionate share of household responsibilities. A majority of working women come home from office work only to start a "second shift" of household work, including food prep, child and elder care, cleaning, shopping, coordinating home services, and family healthcare. Not to mention planning holidays, vacations, birthday parties, and more.

I watched working women be disadvantaged in work environments where the pure mention of personal matters could be a career derailer. Eyes rolled when a woman said she needed to work from home because of a sick child. Hiring decisions were influenced by a woman being a newlywed of childbearing age. The need to take calls or tackle household duties during office hours was often seen as weak or a distraction from work duties.

As my business flourished and our team grew, I saw that the very company that had empowered me at home and work was now enabling me to provide other women with this same flexibility. I continued to build the agency upon the premise that when you provide women with an environment of trust while allowing them the freedom to take care of family duties during the workday without judgment or retribution, you create a win-win situation for all involved. I saw that a culture that promotes balance allows women to be more fully themselves. They feel safe to be vocal, to speak up to let their unique voices be heard. They find themselves more fulfilled within their professional lives as well as at home.

It became a positive equation for the business, our clients as well as our employees. Employees were happier because they were able to lead more balanced lives and often say that they find they perform better at work and feel more productive than they have in prior jobs.

Our clients are grateful (and loyal) because they work with team members who are fulfilled at work and always do their utmost to represent the agency well with their best work. It has also allowed the agency to attract and retain top-notch talent with very low turnover because our employees truly enjoy work-life balance.

I love that a woman can still perform at the top of her game and never question whether she'll be considered less-than because she has to pick up a sick child from school or take a dog to the vet. It's an ambiance of trust that helps women thrive and have careers without sacrificing their personal lives. The virtual agency business model allows each individual to live more wholeheartedly when they show up at work each day. They don't have to pretend that they don't have a life outside of work. There is no inner conflict balancing career and home.

Our mission statement is "To empower smart, passionate women to enjoy their work and life." (And we do employ men. They simply need to embrace our mission!)

I realize that remote work is no longer novel in today's post-COVID climate, but I do believe that an advertising agency that was built upon a platform of empowering women that has been 100% virtual for more than 15 years is certainly something that sets us apart.

When I first made the decision to operate a 100% remote advertising agency, I recognized that we wouldn't be the perfect match for everyone—clients and employees alike. I believed that clients would see the value in the fact that they were hiring experience and talent, not investing in creative office space. That instinct proved true. The resumes of our team and our portfolio of work are what most potential clients are most interested in learning about. Where we office is the least of their worries.

I did learn quickly that not everyone is cut out for remote work. There were times early on when I would find myself wondering, "Where is this person, and how come we haven't heard from her all day?" I believe that there are some people who need the accountability of an office environment to do their best work. There are certain personality types, though, who simply thrive remotely. We started leveraging personality profiling and key interview questions several years back to identify those who would be a good fit and those who would not. We also put procedures in place to keep workers connected and communicating throughout the day. Despite the fact that we have never officed in the same space, we have built a strong corporate culture and a loyal workforce. Employees have told me that they have no intention of ever leaving the company and will retire with us.

Despite our success, there have been plenty of ups and downs throughout the years. I learned that sometimes rapid growth requires major changes in processes and policies and that high revenue does not always mean high profit. I also discovered that the same women I invested in would be there to pick me up and support me when I most needed it, such as going through two major back surgeries or the painful year of splitting my life with my spouse after twenty years together.

Women are incredibly resourceful and resilient. It turns out that building a company upon the pure belief that women are one of a business's most valuable potential commodities is a sound investment.

I was recently asked what advice I would give to my high school self if I could go back in time and speak with her. I don't think that girl could even begin to imagine running a company or leading other companies through rebrands and building successful marketing programs.

Most people are shocked to find out that I was painfully shy as a child. In fact, I had to give my first oral report when I was in seventh grade, and I was so nervous that I hyperventilated and fainted. I knew I needed to combat that intense shyness and fear of people, so I enrolled in drama the following year so I could train to speak in front of people. I went on to continue in theater arts throughout high school and then competed in speech and debate throughout college. I was even a speech communication major. When I tell people today that I'm an introvert they are shocked. "No way. You have to be an extrovert." I explain that my ease in connecting with people is 100% self-taught.

As I reflect upon that shy, insecure high school girl and wonder what advice I would give her, I so wish I could bestow upon her the grace that many of us women develop around middle age. I'd tell her, "Honey, stop worrying so much about what everyone else thinks about you. Comparing yourself to others is wasting fruitless energy. Believe me, those people are far too busy worrying about what everyone else thinks about them to be concerned with you. Worry instead of what YOU really think of yourself. Focus on taking the steps to grow into a woman that YOU admire and hope to someday become. And, P.S., someday you won't even remember most of those high school people's names. You will instead find a tribe of incredible women who will love you for who you are and won't bat an eye at what you are not."

About the Author

Tracy Marlowe believes in the power of women. Early in her career, Tracy worked in offices where women were often considered "less than" for juggling their careers with family matters. In 2008, with a new infant at home, she began building Creative Noggin, a fully remote advertising agency. Her mission was to empower smart, passionate women to do work they enjoyed while balancing their home life with the support of a family-first work environment.

Tracy firmly believes that a woman's potential knows no boundaries. Women are often underestimated yet research shows that women in business consistently outperform their male counterparts. She learned that creating a culture which nurtures women benefits her organization, her clients and the world at large as women are pivotal, influential and support so many around them.

Tracy has over 25 years marketing and branding expertise, having worked with recognizable brands such as Disney, Exxon Mobile and the U.S. Air Force. Her agency, Creative Noggin, specializes in marketing for nonprofits and cause based organizations to include charities, government, zoos, museums, healthcare and foundations. The company has grown from just over $100,000 in sales the first year to upwards of seven million dollars in revenue. The agency donates 5% of its profits annually to causes that support women empowerment and is living proof that a flexible, human-centered workplace is not just good for employees, but also good for business.

Connect with Tracy

Email: tracy@creativenoggin.com

LinkedIn: https://www.linkedin.com/in/tracy-marlowe/

Facebook: https://www.facebook.com/creativenoggin

Instagram: @creative_noggin

Download your free copy of the "5 Most Important Questions to Ask a Marketing Company" by visiting: https://t.ly/sRV7v

EPILOGUE

"The most difficult thing is the decision to act.
The rest is merely tenacity."
– Amelia Earhart

AMELIA EARHART USES THE WORD "merely" before tenacity. But the quality of being tenacious is not "merely" anything. Rather, it comes after that decision to act, and it propels one forward with an unrelenting spirit.

Many people confuse tenacity with stubbornness. However, there's a key difference between the two. Stubbornness is guided by the desire to not change your mind or your position on something. Whereas tenacity is steered by the determination to achieve a goal and being unwilling to give up until you've completed that task.

Lead Like a Woman: Tenacious showcases incredible stories of courage, of determination, of perseverance. The women behind these stories have seen heartache and pain. They've been challenged at every turn by others, by nature, by circumstance.

However, they were and are tenacious. They pursue their dreams and goals relentlessly.

Because of tenacious women, we have WiFi, GPS, and Bluetooth! Hedy Lamarr, a famous film actress, was also an inventor who paved the way for those inventions with the creation of "frequency hopping," a technique for disguising radio transmissions by making the signal jump between different channels in a prearranged pattern. From space stations to coffee filters and from paleontology to social justice, tenacious women have influenced our lives in countless ways.

The women who wrote these chapters are tenacious. Through their tenacity, they've changed lives. It's an honor to share their stories with you.

The *Lead Like a Woman Show* podcast and *The Lead Like a Woman* series of books showcase women who are changing our world through by being tenacious. And it's a privilege to keep reaching more women across the globe. I love to create and share content that empowers others in order to have a more significant impact towards achieving a gender equal world. We have a long way to go, but every tenacious move gets us closer to our goal.

I'm proud to Lead Like a Woman. I'm proud to be tenacious. I hope you are too.

See you soon!

Andrea Heuston

Book Club Questions

SOME OF THE MOST IMPACTFUL DISCUSSIONS I have ever had have been around a table or a friend's living room while sipping beverages and eating snacks with other women. *Lead Like a Woman: TENACIOUS* is perfect for such a discussion!

The best book clubs encourage all voices to participate. Gather everyone in a large space and have a blast discussing everyone's thoughts and experiences with the book. Use the following questions to inspire conversation.

1. Were any of the stories in the book surprising?

2. What did you find inspiring about this book?

3. What was your biggest takeaway from the book?

4. What is the most important piece of advice offered in this book?

5. Who would you recommend this book to?

6. Which story or stories resonated with you the most? Why did they resonate?

7. Which story or stories mirrored any of your experiences in life? How so?

8. What did you like least about the book?

9. What is the significance of the title? Would you have given the book a different title?

10. Have you ever dealt with a similar situation to any of the situations in the book?

11. All of us can be tenacious. What have you done, in your life, that you consider tenacious?

If you got the chance to ask one of the authors of this book one question, which author would you ask and what would your question be?

Made in United States
North Haven, CT
30 May 2024

53086549R10163